MARKETING YOURSELF

MARKETING YOURSELF:

How To Sell Yourself And Get The Jobs You've Always Wanted

DOROTHY LEEDS

GUILD PUBLISHING
LONDON · NEW YORK · SYDNEY · TORONTO

This edition published 1991 by
Guild Publishing by arrangement with
Judy Piatkus (Publishers) Ltd

Copyright © 1991 by Dorothy Leeds

CN 3252

Designed by Sue Ryall

Set in Linotron Plantin by
Phoenix Photosetting, Chatham, Kent
Printed and bound in Great Britain by
Butler & Tanner Ltd, Frome

To **ANNA PEARL ROBERTSON,**

with all my love forever

ACKNOWLEDGEMENTS

With thanks and deep appreciation to:

Sharyn Kolberg, whose diligence, perception and creativity helped make this book a reality. She is a perfect right arm.

Tom Miller, for his guidance, patience and support. He is everything an editor should be, and more.

Jeff Slutsky, the greatest Streetfighter of all, and a pretty good marketer, too.

Ann Wolbrun, for her support, good cheer and dynamite administrative assistance.

All those who so graciously gave of their wisdom and time, especially: Robert Blinder, Susan Boren, James. B. Clemence, Dr. Richard E. Emmert, Joe Gandolpho, Joe Girard, Roberts T. Jones, John Kelman, Aven Kerr, William Olsten, Judd Saviskas, Ellen Schneider, Arthur Denny Scott, Martin Shafiroff, Robert Shook, Steve Stein, George Walther, and Walter F. Whitt.

The Sales & Marketing Executives of Greater New York and Ed Flanagan for paving the way.

Special appreciation to my family, Nonny, Ian and Laura, for their continued love, support and forbearance.

CONTENTS

INTRODUCTION

W hat is the ultimate job seeker's fantasy? Everyone I asked told me, 'Getting paid well for doing what I love to do.'

Why aren't we all living out our job fantasies? Because, up until now, the way to get the jobs we want has been a mystery. I have written this book to turn mystery into mastery.

No matter what kind of job you're looking for, no matter what your experience (or lack of it), no matter where you are right now, this book will show you exactly how to get the job of your choice – with the salary, perks and benefits you deserve. All you have to do is learn how to sell and market yourself – the two most essential skills and techniques you'll need for getting a job in the 1990s and beyond.

The purpose of this book is to teach you those sales and marketing skills and show you exactly how they apply to getting the job of your choice.

My own expertise in sales and marketing is the fruit of 15 years of study, experience and training. I have made my living passing this knowledge on to others. I have built up an extensive marketing organis- ation of my own, and in the course of speaking and consulting all over the country, I've trained over 20,000 executives and salespeople.

Having had five successful careers (so far) in my life, I'm an expert on the subject of how to get the job of your choice. I have an insider's under- standing of what it's like to go out and look for a job.

When I first started out, I studied other successful job seekers. What was their secret? Some were better educated than I was, but others weren't. Some had nicer clothes or were more charming or had more advanced technical skills. Their only common trait, the one area in which they all stood above the crowd, was their *ability to sell and market themselves*.

But the most revealing discovery was that these people had no innate sales and marketing abilities. They taught themselves: they read, practised, and, through trial and error, mastered the techniques that got them started on their successful career paths. What I learned enabled me to get a high-level position in the competitive world of advertising – with no prior experience or training in that field!

My goal in writing this book is to eliminate the 'trial and error' part of the process for you. Here, in one complete, easy to follow, step-by-step guide, you'll find all the information you need to fulfil your own career dreams, goals and ambitions.

I didn't rely on my experience alone for this information. I went to the experts – company chairmen, managing directors, personnel managers, senior executives – to find out what they look for in a potential employee. I asked the top sales and marketing professionals in a variety of fields what made them so good at what they do. I studied economic trends, population growth, and the key jobs for this decade and beyond.

By combining this information with the sales and marketing techniques in this book, you'll be among the top contenders for any job you go after.

Marketing Yourself is divided into five sections:

Part 1: How to Get the Job of Your Choice: Sell, Don't Settle
- Get the inside track to success by selling and marketing yourself
- Learn how your attitudes and emotional responses to sales and marketing may be holding you back, and what to do about it
- Build the confidence you need to go out and sell yourself

Part 2: The Success Factors: Your Ten Most Marketable Skills
- Ten qualities and personal characteristics every employer is looking for – universal skills which will make you an ideal candidate for any job you choose, plus examples, quizzes and assessments to help you measure and improve your own Success Factors.

Part 3: Know Your Product
- Learn the real reasons why people get employed and how to market your 'product' accordingly and show employers you've got what they need
- Make your personal job search easier by specifying and clarifying your own career goals
- Sell yourself successfully using your most marketable skills and accomplishments – whether you've had a lifetime of career success or never had a job before.

Part 4: Know Your Market
- Keep yourself motivated, activated and on-target by developing your own personal Marketing Plan
- Recognise current economic trends, how they affect you and the way you work
- Discover 30 of the hottest job markets in the country today and what skills you need to get them.

Part 5: Closing the Sale
- Use inside secrets from top sales professionals to 'clinch the deal'
- Put step-by-step marketing procedures and specific sales techniques to work for you:
  - Locate the people who most want to employ you
  - Make employers the offers they can't refuse
  - Sell yourself effectively in any interview situation
  - Eliminate key areas of interviewing anxiety
  - Negotiate for more than money
  - Get the jobs you really want.

This book was written for each of you, individually. Because the job search is so unique to each of us (we all have different goals, ambitions and priorities), the book contains personal assessment quizzes and individualised worksheets to make each step particular to your specific needs. It's designed to be a guide to your future, a handbook of practical information and profitable strategies for success throughout your working lifetime.

It's also designed to assure you that it is possible to build the career of your choice. It doesn't matter how old you are now or whether you're looking for your first or your twenty-first job, the journey is the same. If you plan well, and travel with an open mind and a flexible attitude, your trip will be both pleasurable and satisfying. Unexpected detours abound, and you may have to alter your route as you go. Or you may find a more interesting, less travelled path and decide you'd rather explore this instead.

Marketing Yourself will help you build the skills necessary to deal with whatever career changes and choices you face now and will face in the years to come – if you want to move up the corporate ladder, or if you want to change careers mid-stream. Selling and marketing skills will help you to be prepared for unexpected change, and to have more confidence in yourself and your abilities. You will learn to measure your value and use that knowledge to get what you want.

At the beginning of each chapter you'll find a basic principle of sales and marketing that encapsulates the significance of the information that follows. These 28 principles will provide you with the basis of a strong and practical understanding of sales and marketing.

I guarantee that if you learn *and apply* these principles to the job search, you'll gain the confidence, self-knowledge, and skills to pursue the career you've always wanted, and to be a happier and wealthier participant in the workforce of today and tomorrow.

PART ONE

HOW TO GET THE JOB
OF YOUR CHOICE:

Sell, Don't Settle

1

MARKETING YOURSELF:
The Ultimate Job Seeker's Skill

'Marketing success depends on the quality of the product
plus the ability of the salesperson'

I f you're looking for an ordinary, run-of-the-mill job you don't have to read this book. It doesn't take any special skill to get that kind of a job. But if you're serious about finding the right job for you, the one that will make you happy and pay you what you deserve, it's time to get down to business – the business of selling yourself.

If you're looking for a magic formula for getting the job of your choice, look no further; there is no magic formula.

There is a secret, but it's not magic. It's learning and specific skills and techniques that successful salespeople have been using for years, and applying those concepts to your search for a better job.

The sales and marketing techniques you'll learn in this book will help you to:

- reach the people who would be most interested in employing you
- understand the real reasons people 'buy' – and why employers will want to 'buy' what you have to sell
- build the career you've always dreamed of having
- ask for more and get it.

Whether you're selling carpets or computers, hammers or hosiery, trumpets or tractors, the principles of sales and marketing remain the same. And it is these same principles that you'll need when you're 'selling' your skills and abilities to potential employers. Once you learn these sales and marketing techniques you'll have the strong foundation you need to pursue the career you choose.

No person is an island, and it doesn't do you much good to be strong,

3

confident and talented if you keep it to yourself. If you want to be success-ful in following your chosen career path, you're going to have to let the rest of the world know about it. You're going to have to sell and market yourself.

BIRTH OF A SALESPERSON

Success in today's changing workplace depends on action, not reaction. You have to do more than send out CVs in response to job ads. There are many intelligent, creative people seeking challenging, well-paying jobs. You have to become a salesperson if you don't want to be left behind.

The most significant challenge job applicants face today is improving their salespersonship. The secret of getting ahead, of obtaining the competitive edge, is your ability to persuade potential employers that *they need you*. That's what selling and marketing are all about.

Selling is simply showing someone else how your product or service will help him or her fill a need or solve a problem. Marketing is the process of getting a product or service from the seller to the buyer. Learning to market yourself is learning how to connect the product (you) with the buyers (employers) you seek. Buyers are looking at an overall package when they make their decisions. How you sell and market that package can make the difference between you and the competition, which is get-ting stronger all the time.

It doesn't matter if you're old or young, if you're just graduating from college or if you're changing careers after 20 years on the job; I'll show you how to discover your strong points and emphasise your assets and how to have the career you've always dreamed about having.

What you are going to do from here until the end of this book is to:

- identify your strengths, talents and interests
- increase your self-confidence as you discover your value to others
- become a salesperson and learn how to market and promote yourself, using your personal assets as the foundation for a lifetime of career choices.

This process will not end when you finish the book; it is a process to conti-nue for a lifetime, and one that will expand and grow as you do.

THE SELLERS AND THE BUYERS

When an employer decides to offer you a job, he's buying your talents, your technical abilities, your appearance, your personality – in fact every-thing about you is part of the package. In the business of selling yourself, just as in every other business, your primary objective is to persuade companies or individuals to purchase your product or service. Your success rate will increase dramatically the more sales and marketing techniques you learn.

This isn't a gimmick I invented to sell more books. This is a system that really works. When I use the terms 'sale' or 'selling' throughout this book, I'm really referring to the entire job search process. The term 'buyer' refers to potential employees. I've used examples of sales and marketing success stories, and translated these principles into actions you can take to pursue the career of your choice successfully.

No Hard Sell in the New Age

Why is it that selling and salespeople have developed such a shady reputation over the years? A successful salesperson used to be a charmer, someone who could sweet talk you out of your last pound, and an eager buying public welcomed his promises of health, wealth and happiness even at a high price.

The 'hard sell' has been around for hundreds of years. It used to be that a salesperson would do anything – lie, cheat, bamboozle – anything to make a sale. What has happened to the hard sell in the new age? Selling isn't what it used to be. The hard sell is losing its grip as new concepts in selling have emerged. There is a kinder, gentler type of salesperson, who asks questions and listens instead of bulldozing his or her way through a sale. Lying and cheating are too easily detectable these days; honesty is the best policy in the information age.

So why do so many people shudder at the thought of having to go out and sell anything at all, no less themselves? We're shy. We're modest. We're embarrassed to talk about ourselves. But think of it this way: if you owned a business, would you simply open a store, sit there and wait for customers to come to you? If you did, you'd go out of business in a very short time. You'd have to tell someone about your product. You'd have to get the word out. And if the *owner* of the business was reluctant to sell, who else would do it for you?

If you picture a salesperson as an old-time huckster you're not going to be comfortable learning the sales techniques you'll need to make your career dreams a reality. Selling is an art and once learned, it can be of benefit to you in every area of your life.

A 'new' salesperson has emerged in the business world because the customer has changed. People are more aware than they used to be and are not as gullible or as easily convinced. So the new salesperson sees him or herself as someone whose purpose is to help others solve their problems.

That's exactly what you're doing when you're looking for a job. You're trying to match up your talents and abilities with an employer who has a problem you can solve or a need you can fill. The same techniques that sales and marketing experts are using successfully for their products can be applied – with equal success – to the job search process, and this book will show you how to do it.

THE CAREER ENTREPRENEUR

When Josh was a little boy he wanted to be a farmer. As he grew older he began to realise the difficulties facing farmers today. But he couldn't deny his love of the land, or give up his dream altogether. So he researched the 'dying' agricultural market, chose his area of study, and became an agricultural engineer. Today he studies and invents new and improved plants that will strengthen farmers' productivity and profits. Josh took advantage of a growing field even in an industry that's supposedly in decline.

Josh made a successful career choice because he had an eye on the future. He chose a field based on a growing technology.

This was a smart marketing move. Josh already has the makings of the new entrepreneur. An entrepreneur is someone who sees an opportunity, weighs up all the alternatives, considers the risks and takes decisive action. The smart employee of the 1990s is a career entrepreneur. If you want to be among the successful, you have to weigh your alternatives, consider the risks and take decisive action in the business of planning and promoting your life and your life's work. Other people may present you with opportunities, but you're the only one who can take action one way or the other. You're the boss of your own life, whether you work for someone else or not.

As you develop a career marketing strategy, whether you work for a large company or work for yourself, you'll need that entrepreneurial spirit. You'll need to manage yourself as if you were running a small business. The information in this book provides you with the secrets to market yourself successfully in any field you choose. You need to have an aggressive marketing plan, just as any small business would. You need to know your 'product' inside and out, and how to bring that product to the buying public. You need to know where your industry or field of interest is heading, so that your 'product' remains a marketable commodity in a rapidly changing world. And you need to have the skills of salesmanship to convince the buyer of the value of the product.

THE SPIRIT OF THE 90s

There is a new spirit that's revitalising the way we work in the West. It has nothing to do with mysticism or spiritual rebirth. It has to do with what we want out of work – what we choose to do with our lives, and how, when and where we choose to do it. This new spirit tells us to be proud of who we are, and to go after what we want.

It's in this spirit that marketing prowess is becoming the hallmark of career success in the 90s. After reading this book you need never be anxious or frightened about getting a job again! The promise I make is a promise for your future: marketing yourself will bring you a lifetime's reward of confidence, fulfilment and career success.

2

*T*HE SALES READINESS QUIZ

'Attitude is more important than aptitude for sales and marketing success'

D o you have a 'sales personality'? Are you 'market oriented' and 'sales minded'? According to the experts, those are the qualities you'll need most to get the job of your choice.

This is not a test of your knowledge of sales techniques. It's a quiz to evaluate your sales personality, as well as your attitude about selling in general.

Be honest with yourself when you take this quiz. Go with your instinct – how you would most likely react in the given situation, what you really think – not what you think the answer should be. You can't fail this quiz. It's meant only as a guide and a reference by which to judge your sales readiness.

Don't be concerned if you don't score as highly as you'd like to. Read this book, do the worksheets and follow the suggestions you find here, then take the quiz again. I guarantee you won't be disappointed a second time!

SALES READINESS QUIZ

1. You are planning a holiday with a friend. You want to go to Paris and your friend wants to go on a cruise. Would you:

    A   Talk dynamically about Paris and what you love about it
    B   Debate or ignore every reason he/she presents for going on the cruise
    C   Try and find out what it is about the cruise that appeals to your friend most

2. What is the most difficult aspect of getting a job?

    A   Finding the right job opportunities
    B   Asking for the job at the interview
    C   Calling to make the appointment

3. When you picture a salesperson in your mind's eye, do you see:

    A   A person who is trying to help you solve a problem
    B   An arm-twisting used-car salesperson
    C   A smooth persuader whose main motive is to sell you his or her product or service

4. Your main goal at a job interview is:

    A   To get the job
    B   To get as much information as possible
    C   To ask questions

5. When you solve a major problem at work, do you:

    A   Go in and ask for a raise
    B   Write it down and bring it up at Performance Appraisal time
    C   Give it little notice and assume your boss is keeping an appreciative eye on all your accomplishments

6. You are planning to buy three pairs of expensive shoes in a small boutique. Do you:

    A   Pay for them
    B   Ask at the beginning if they'll give a discount if you buy all three
    C   After trying on shoes for three hours, say I might buy if you give a discount for buying three pairs

7. The last time someone said no to you, did you:

    A   Ask why he or she said no
    B   Take the no as an irrevocable decision
    C   Keep trying to persuade him or her to say yes

8. In a group of very aggressive, talkative people, do you:

    A   Hold you own comfortably
    B   Sit back timidly content to listen
    C   Speak up occasionally because you don't want to be left out

9. If someone asked you to describe your best feature, would you:

   A Talk non-stop for hours
   B Blush and not know where to start
   C Discuss briefly two or three admirable traits

10. If you hear about a job opening do you:

    A Send a CV
    B Call personnel to get more information
    C Try to contact the person you'd actually be working for

11. How would you prepare for a job interview:

    A Role play with friends or colleagues
    B Develop a list of questions to ask
    C Think about what you'll be asked and prepare some answers

12. When sending out a letter with your CV to a prospective employer do you:

    A Send a standard letter
    B Send no letter
    C Write a tailored letter for each job

13. If you call a prospective employer and he or she immediately says 'We're not hiring today,' what do you think is the reason?

    A The employer took an instant dislike to you
    B It's not the right time
    C He or she doesn't have a good reason to talk to you

14. If you were selling computers and needed customers would you:

    A Call up all your friends
    B Attend a seminar on 'Computer Basics for Small Business Owners'
    C Open the phone book and start calling

15. You have applied for a job you really want and have been turned down by personnel. Would you:

    A Call and try to get another appointment
    B Accept the decision and try another company
    C Try to find out who you would be reporting to and make an appointment directly with that person

16. Why do you think people 'buy'?

    A   Because it makes them feel good
    B   It's based on a logical decision
    C   Because they like the salesperson

17. You are going on an important interview. Do you:

    A   Research the company
    B   Decide you'll bluff your way through it
    C   Figure you'll ask questions to learn what you need to know at the interview

18. A friend gives you a referral. Do you:

    A   Take the name and number and say, 'I'll call next week'
    B   Take the name and number and call immediately
    C   Ask your friend for more information about the job and the boss

19. Why is listening such an important part of the sales process?

    A   You get important information
    B   You find out the hidden concerns
    C   It shows that you care

20. What is the best way to stay in control during a sales presentation or a job interview?

    A   Always have a planned question at the ready
    B   Keep talking in a very persuasive manner
    C   Answer every objection or concern that is raised

21. At the end of a job interview, do you:

    A   Say thank you and leave
    B   Ask for the job
    C   Ask when you'll be hearing from them

22. You've been searching for a job for 6 months, and have been rejected 20 times. Do you:

    A   Get angry and take it out on friends and family
    B   Begin to doubt your own abilities
    C   Re-evaluate your interviewing skills

23. In an interview situation, which would you see as a strong signal of acceptance:

    A   If the interviewer asks, 'When can you start?'
    B   If the interviewer says, 'This would be your desk'
    C   If the interview goes on for a long time

24. You get a letter from a satisfied customer commending you, or from a colleague complimenting your performance. Do you:

    A   Show it to your family, friends and colleagues
    B   Acknowledge it, feel good, and stash it away
    C   Make copies and send it to your boss, her boss, your department head, even the managing director or chairman

25. Who do you think gets to the top in most organisations:

    A   People who work the hardest
    B   People who fit in to the corporate mould
    C   People who sell themselves most effectively

SCORING

1. A = 3 B = 1 C = 5

The worst way to try and 'sell' anything is to ignore or argue with the other person (B). You only hurt their feelings or make them want to cling stubbornly to their own position. Talking dynamically about Paris may help you out (A), but the real secret to selling is to appeal to what the other person wants or needs. By finding out what's most appealing about the idea of a cruise, (C) you'll know what the other person really wants. Then if he or she says, 'There's lots of dancing on board ship,' for instance, you'll know you can counter that with a list of places to go dancing in Paris.

2. A = 3 B = 5 C = 3

Even the most experienced salespeople sometimes have difficulty 'asking for the order'. (B) When you're in an interview (the ultimate sales situation), an essential sales skill is knowing how to be assertive without being aggressive. Finding job opportunities (A) is not difficult if you take advantage of research tools available in the papers, the library, and personal contacts. And calling to make the appointment (C), also an important skill, is not difficult if you utilise the three Ps: patience, practice and perseverance.

3. A = 5 B = 0 C = 1

Your inner picture of what a salesperson is will greatly influence your ability to succeed in today's job market. If you see an arm-twisting salesperson (B), you won't feel very good about having to sell yourself. If you see a person who's trying to help you solve your problems (A), that's the kind of salesperson you'll be during your job hunt. Smooth per-suaders (C) will probably always do well in this world, but will always come in second to someone who is genuinely concerned with solving other people's problems.

4. A = 5 B = 5 C = 5

All three of these answers are good. You want to come away with a job offer so that it is your choice whether or not you take the job (A); you want to get as much information as possible so you can make a smart decision about the job (B); and you want to go in prepared to ask questions (C) in order to accomplish A and B.

5. A = 5 B = 3 C = 1

If you go right in and ask for a raise then you're sales oriented and inter-ested in promoting your value (A). This is the best approach and is in step with today's more assertive approach to life. Waiting for performance appraisal time is good (B), but that may be a long time off. Our phil-osophy is that it's more important to keep yourself in the eye of the organ-isation, and you do this by letting them know when you've done something valuable. If you give it little notice (C), no one else will notice it either and you're definitely not in keeping with the marketplace. If you don't sell yourself nobody else will.

6. A = 1 B = 3 C = 5

Negotiation is an important selling skill. The best time to ask for a discount is after they've invested time showing their wares (C). At that point, they'd rather give you a deal than lose the sale. You get three points for being able to ask for a discount when you come in (B). You're on the right track, but you don't want to tip your hand at the beginning. You get one point (A) for being successful enough to be able to pay for three expensive pairs of shoes.

7. A = 5   B = 1   C = 3

It's important to know why someone says 'no' (A) if you want to get a 'yes' the next time. It might even tell you how to proceed to change the 'no' to a 'yes' this time. If you keep trying (C), it means you're not easily dissuaded, and have enough confidence in yourself to try again. If you take every 'no' as an irrevocable decision (B), you're not being realistic, or giving yourself a chance to find out what your mistake might have been.

8. A = 5   B = 2   C = 3

Congratulations on holding your own (A) and feeling comfortable about it. Competition for jobs will be great, and the better your communications skills, the easier you'll find it to sell yourself, and the better your chances of getting the jobs you want. Speaking up occasionally (C) gets you three points for realising that you need to at least make an effort to participate. You get two points for listening (B) because you may gain valuable information, but you'll need to learn to jump in and hold your own if you're going to compete in the job market.

9. A = 1   B = 3   C = 5

Talking non-stop about your product (in this case yourself) is not a very effective sales technique (A). Your customers will see you as being pushy or unconcerned with their welfare. If you blush and don't know where to start (B) it means you're unprepared for the question. You wouldn't start selling cars without knowing anything about them. You'd prepare yourself for the questions your customers will most likely ask. If your answer was (C), it shows you think enough of yourself to be able to discuss your good qualities without being obsessive or obnoxious.

10. A = 1   B = 2   C = 5

If you follow the techniques of successful salespeople, you'll take the initiative, be more assertive, and try to go directly to the person who will make the final decision (C). Since you've heard about the position, use your source to get your foot in the door: 'Johnny Jones suggested I call . . .' Calling personnel to get more information might be somewhat helpful (B); it shows that you're willing to do some research. If you just send a CV to personnel (A), you're not taking advantage of your inside knowledge.

11. A = 5   B = 5   C = 5

This is another question where all three answers are good. Doing well at job interviews takes skill, and the way to build a skill is to be well prepared and practise, practise, practise. So all three answers will be helpful to you.

12. A = 2   B = 0   C = 5

Sending a CV by itself (B) with no covering letter at all tells a potential employer that you have no special interest in him or his company. The sales-oriented approach is to let the employer know why it is in his best interest to read the CV and call you in for an interview. You do this by sending a letter tailored specifically for him (C). Sending a standard letter is almost as bad as no letter at all (A).

13. A = 1   B = 3   C = 5

In selling terms, you've encountered 'sales resistance' in this situation. Sales resistance occasionally occurs when the customer doesn't like the salesperson (A), but in this case you hadn't been speaking long enough for the employer to truly dislike you (unless you were rude or obnoxious). It's possible that the employer was busy and you caught her at a bad time (B). But the most common reason for resistance is that the salesperson hasn't established the value of the product or service (C) – in other words, hasn't presented a strong enough reason for the customer to buy (or for the employer to keep talking to you). If this happens often when you call, it means you need to change your initial approach.

14. A = 4   B = 5   C = 1

Calling all your friends (A) is an excellent way to start. Networking is one of the best ways to find buyers for your product. Attending a seminar for new business owners (B) shows you have a strong sales sensibility. People who attend such a seminar are 'qualified' buyers – they're definitely in the market for your product, so your chances of making a sale here are very good. Just opening the phone book (C) and making calls may bring you a few customers, but you'll probably waste most of your time and effort. In the job search, the more qualified buyers you reach, the better your chances of getting the job you want.

15. A = 3   B = 0   C = 5

If you have been turned down by personnel and just accept their decision (B), you are too easily discouraged. Successful salespeople learn to accept rejection, and go on to the next opportunity. If you go directly to the decision maker (C), you'll be demonstrating sales initiative and persistence, both necessary and desirable qualities for the job search process. Trying to get another appointment through personnel (B) is not as effective, but does show you're resilient and not easily put off.

16. A = 5   B = 1   C = 3

Emotions play a very strong part in both the selling and the hiring process. People 'buy' (or employ) for emotional reasons (A); the product fulfils a need or desire they have. That's why in order to sell yourself to an employer, you'll have to show him how you'll solve his problems or fulfil his needs. People also buy from people they like, trust and respect (C). You can't *make* someone like you, but you can show that you are a person worthy of trust and respect. Logic almost always plays a lesser role in the decision-making process (B).

17. A = 5   B = 0   C = 3

Although asking questions (C) is an essential part of the interviewing process, most people are impressed by what you *already* know about them. Take time before you go on any 'sales call' to learn as much as you can about the company, and the person you're going to see (A). You'll stand out from other applicants. If you try to bluff your way through it without having made any preparations (B), you put yourself at a definite disadvantage – not only do you know nothing about the company to start with, but you won't even know what questions you should be asking or what you need to know about the job.

18. A = 1   B = 3   C = 5

The best answer in this case is to ask your friend for as much information as you can get before you make the call (C). You want to try and find out something about the person you'll be calling (who they are, what their position is in the company, etc), what the job is like, and why the vacancy exists. Your friend may not be able to fill you in completely, but may give you enough to prepare you for the call. Calling immediately (B) shows that you have initiative, but you'd be better off doing research about the company first. If you say, 'I'll call next week' (A), you're probably just putting it off, and may lose the opportunity.

19. A = 5   B = 5   C = 5

All three answers are true. There's an old sales saying that goes 'Customers don't care how much you know until they know how much you care.' At a job interview the interviewer wants to know that you care about the job and the company (C). Of course you get important factual

16

information by listening (A), but you also find out the hidden concerns of the individual interviewer (B) when you listen carefully. These hidden concerns are the real reasons why you will or won't get the job.

20. A = 5   B = 1   C = 3

There is another sales secret that says 'The person who asks the question controls the conversation.' That's why you want to go into the interview with a series of planned questions (A) – so you can remain in control of the situation, and be sure you get all the information you need to make a smart decision. What you think is talking in a persuasive manner (B) may come across as conceited or pushy. Without asking questions, you could end up talking for hours and never satisfy any of the employer's real concerns. Clearly answering objections or concerns (C) is essential to a successful interview, but it doesn't give you the same control that asking questions does.

21. A = 1   B = 5   C = 3

It's important that you 'ask for the sale' or, in this case, the job (B). Ask in a pleasant civil way so that you don't turn people off. Saying thank you and leaving (A) is not going to help you get the job unless you're the most sought after person in the world. Asking when you'll be hearing from her (C) shows a little more assertiveness, and is better than just saying thanks and leaving, but more than likely you'll be told 'We have several candidates to choose from, we'll call you.' You're not going to get very far with that, so its always best to ask a closing question.

22. A = 0   B = 1   C = 5

The best answer here is to re-evaluate your interviewing skills (C). Twenty interviews can give you a lot of good information about the different types of situations that may arise. Go over your experiences and ask yourself what you did right, and what can be improved. If you begin to doubt your own abilities, it means you're taking rejection too personally. A rejection may have nothing to do with you personally, and you're letting that belief get in your way of achieving the success you deserve. Getting angry, at yourself or at anyone else (A), doesn't improve your skills or your chances at the next interview. Don't give up trying; the next interview could be the one you've been waiting for!

23. A = 3   B = 5   C = 1

Most people take a long interview as a definite sign of interest (C). In fact, this often signifies nothing more than a disorganised interviewer, someone who doesn't really know what he's looking for. Don't assume that an hour-long interview means you'll be on the short list. If, however, the interviewer starts to visualise you in the job, and consistently refers to 'your' desk, 'your' colleagues etc (B), it's a pretty good clue that there is a strong interest there. 'When can you start' (A) is a possible sign of interest, but it may also indicate that the employer is in urgent need of someone and may not be able to wait until you're available.

24. A = 3   B = 1   C = 5

Do you feel comfortable enough to take hold of your future and make sure the right people see what others think of you? Since only the rich and famous have agents or public relations firms, we have to take over that role for ourselves. The best answer is (C). Showing the letter to your friends and colleagues (A) will make you feel better and perhaps add to your reputation, but may not do much where your boss is concerned. Feeling good is always nice (B), but why pass over opportunities to promote yourself?

25. A = 3   B = 4   C = 5

Although we're in the middle of the information age, we're also at the beginning of the age of marketing. Even our MPs have to sell themselves if they want to get elected. You must be well versed in sales and marketing skills to get ahead (C). Fitting into the corporate mould is and will continue to be important (B), but it is decreasing in value as work becomes less structured in many situations. Hard workers (A) are not to be discounted – but they are not necessarily the people who get ahead. In a small or newly organised company this may be the case, but unless other people know how hard you work, or unless you fit in with the rest of the team, your hard work will not always be appreciated.

WHAT YOUR SCORE MEANS

95–120 points

Good for you! You've scored high in sales readiness which means you're one step ahead of the competition already. You have a positive attitude towards selling and a personality that makes you a natural for marketing yourself.

70–95 points

You are well on your way toward the sales and marketing orientation required for success in today's job market. You're thinking along the right lines and, with just a little improvement, there'll be no stopping you!

45–70 points

You're not quite at the level you should be, but you're getting there. It would help you to be a bit more assertive and to have more confidence in yourself and your abilities. All it takes is a shift in attitude and a willingness to learn. You're on the right track.

Less than 45 points

You need to revaluate your attitudes and perceptions regarding sales and marketing. Doing the exercises and following the principles put forth in this book will be a great help in improving your sales readiness and increasing your marketing power.

3

SOLD ON YOURSELF

'If you don't believe in the value of your product, no one else will either'

SELLING YOURSELF WITHOUT SELLING OUT

Do you have an adverse reaction when I talk about selling yourself? Are you still thinking in terms of the huckster we talked about in Chapter 1? Do you think that selling yourself some how implies a loss of dignity or a weakness of character? Or perhaps you think you're so good that you don't need to sell yourself? I hope you answered no to all these questions.

You don't become successful by sitting back and waiting for good things to happen to you. Marketing yourself is the only way to spread the word. Do you think Michael Jackson or Madonna never did any marketing? Or Annita Roddick? Or anyone else at the top of their profession? They all had to sell themselves to get where they are today.

And as for loss of dignity or weakness of character, this is a very distorted notion of what selling yourself is all about. Selling yourself does *not* mean selling out. Those people who sell out are those who *don't follow their dreams*; those who give up because the path they've chosen turns out to be a little rockier than they had first imagined.

When you were a child, people probably often asked you, 'What do you want to be when you grow up?' You would have answered with a clear (if temporary) vision of your future self – doctor, dancer, train driver, astronaut, movie star, prime minister.

If someone had asked instead, 'What do you think you can be when you grow up?', would you have answered differently?

Probably not. Because when we are young we can envisage ourselves as we want to be: singing on stage, reading the news on television or

20

playing on the centre court at Wimbledon. We can imagine ourselves performing delicate brain surgery or designing the world's longest suspension bridge. We can picture ourselves strong, confident, capable, and unafraid. The gap between what we want and what we think we can do is very small.

For most of us, this gap begins to widen as we grow older. The first time someone tells us 'you're not clever enough' or 'tall enough' or 'girls can't do that', we are astounded by this news and shrug it off as just another mistaken adult notion. The second and third times, however, we begin to doubt ourselves, and after a while we believe what we are told. We build up an inventory of 'cannots', 'should nots' and 'it's never been done befores'. We lose our certainty, and the clear pictures we had as children become cloudy and fade.

Sometimes you have to go back to go ahead. This book is about going back to those visions of what you really wanted to do, and replacing the old inventory of negatives with an objective and positive assessment of your own talents and achievements. You are this country's finest resource, harbouring a wealth of untapped or undervalued potential waiting only to be discovered.

Most people seem to think that you can't be true to yourself and what you want to do, and sell yourself at the same time. I'm here to tell you that it is possible, in fact it is absolutely necessary, to do both.

I believe in truth in advertising. I'm not telling you to learn sales and marketing skills so that you can spout a lot of hype about yourself and fool someone into giving you a job you can't do. I'm encouraging you to add salespersonship to your other skills so that you can have the career you want, and use your basic talents to your best potential.

Instead of going after what we want, we have been taking what we can get. A very famous book called *Think and Grow Rich* written by Napoleon Hill, contains the statement, 'Ninety-eight out of every hundred people working for wages today are in the positions they hold because they lacked the definiteness of decision to plan a definite position, and the knowledge of how to choose an employer.'

You don't have to be among those 98 unhappy people. By setting goals that are important to you and that will make you happy, you will have the 'definiteness of decision.' And by following the marketing concepts in this book, you'll know how to choose an employer.

The success of any sales and marketing effort depends to a large extent on the salesperson's expectations. If you go into a situation convinced that you will fail – that you won't make the sale, or won't get the job – you probably won't.

Most of us have been programmed to equate mistakes with failure. We use the fact that we have made a mistake as proof positive that we are unworthy or unable to attain success. We tend to fall back into old attitudes when dealing with new situations, and we often rely on the conditioned response which says 'Oops! Sorry! This can't be done!' We believe this inner voice, and give up before we have even tried.

Belief in failure can become a conditioned response, but so can belief in *success*! Olympic athletes train more than their bodies to earn that gold medal; they prepare their minds as well. Before they begin a race they envisage their performance. They rehearse their success before it happens.

Paint a clear, detailed picture of what you want to accomplish for yourself, and then take each small step necessary to follow it through. Barbara Sher, in her book, *Wishcraft: How to Get What You Really Want*, says, 'Most of us have a distorted notion of how things actually get done in this world. We think that accomplishment only comes from great deeds. Great deeds are made up of small, steady actions, and it is these that you must learn to value and sustain.'

Your ability to succeed in selling yourself doesn't depend on what has happened in your past, but on how you see your future. Convince yourself that you will be successful and you'll convince others as well.

LEARNING TO ROOT FOR YOURSELF

There is one aspect of successful selling that is just as important as any skill or technique you can learn. No one can hope to be a good salesperson unless he has a strong belief in the product he's selling. Enthusiasm is catching. If you have a positive attitude about yourself and your ability to do the job, the potential employer will feel this too. As every salesperson can confirm, even the most successful of them fail to make a sale sometimes. But as Eleanor Roosevelt (wife of Franklin Roosevelt) once said, 'No one can make you feel inferior without your consent.'

You're probably not going to get every job offer you go after. But don't let anyone put you down or make you feel inadequate. Only you can let that happen. You may feel rejected or criticised, but see it for what it is: a temporary refusal. A 'no' in one place is equal to a 'yes' waiting for you somewhere else.

A friend once went through a particularly tough interview and was then turned down for a job she really wanted. Two days later she received a phone call. The employer had had time to think back over her interview and asked if she would come in and talk to him again. He was in a much better mood this time around and she was offered the job. He had simply changed his mind. Employers are human too; they have their good days and their bad days, just like you.

You can't know the future. Recently, I was looking for a salesperson for my office. There were two candidates I really liked, and I had a difficult time making up my mind. As it turned out, the person I employed had to leave the job after only three weeks due to personal problems. I immediately called the second candidate, and offered her the job.

So don't take a 'no' as a permanent, scarring rejection or an indicator of things to come. Go into each situation feeling confident about yourself and giving an impression of being enthusiastic about the job – but not desperate for it. A buyer is always suspicious of a salesperson who is obviously desperate to make a sale. Even if you're down to your last few pounds, never act needy. Every time you set out to 'make a sale', remind yourself that you are a unique, special individual with a lot of talent and a genuine contribution to make.

But first, a word about the real competition

In searching for a job or career opportunity, you are often advised to take note of the fierce competition, that you must stand out from the crowd, and achieve that competitive edge.

There is no disputing the numbers. There will always be a certain number of people applying for the same job. Sometimes these numbers will be great and there are times, when you may get discouraged and begin to think you haven't got what it takes. You may begin to measure yourself against those around you, to see everyone else as being better than you are. You might occasionally feel inferior, and therefore not worthy or deserving of success. Perhaps you've had failures in the past, and you point to them and say, 'Experience tells me I'm not capable.' It's important, however, to keep things in perspective. You may feel that you're not capable, but remember this is *not a fact*, it's only the way you *feel*. Most of us have experienced these kinds of feelings at some time or another.

Keep in mind one of the most important principles of sales and marketing: *if you don't believe in the value of your product, no one else will either*.

This doesn't mean you're not concerned with the competition. You are. But the competition you need to be most concerned about comes from within. According to Joe Girard, listed in the *Guinness Book of World Records* as the 'World's Number One New Car Salesman', 'Before you can sell yourself successfully to others – and thus sell your ideas, your wishes, your needs, your ambitions, your skills, your experience, your products and services – you must be absolutely sold on yourself: 100%.'

Don't let the negative voices within you compete with your talents and abilities. You can gain the 'competitive edge' over these voices within that say you're unable to do this or that, that you're 'not creative' or 'have no mathematical ability' or 'can't speak in front of people.'

These voices can be very convincing. A voice says, 'You have no mathematical ability' and you give up trying to balance the chequebook. Albert Einstein failed algebra in school. Did this prove he had no mathematical abilities? If he had believed that was true, the Theory of Relativity might never have been born.

The 'you don't have to be Einstein' equation

Philip, a friend, once came to me in a panic. His supervisor had resigned and Philip had a chance to go after the position. This was the opportunity he had been waiting for. There was one hitch, however. As head of the department, he would be required to present semi-annual reports to the board of directors. Philip had always admired his supervisor's presentations and believed he could 'never get up in front of those people and speak the way she did'. Philip didn't feel he could sell himself for this position.

He came to me to ask for help in public speaking. I knew I could help him, give him voice and speech exercises, and help build his confidence. But I also knew he would never be able to sell himself believing that he had to 'speak the way she did'. Philip was competing with an exaggerated image of someone whose abilities he admired. He could do a fine job himself, but until he replaced the old image with a belief in his own ability and individuality, he would always fall short of his expectations.

You act on your beliefs. If you believe you can't, you can't. Subtract one little apostrophe and one small letter of the alphabet and you can change your life. Remember this equation: CAN'T − 'T = CAN. You don't have to be Einstein to appreciate its simplicity.

When I introduced Philip to the 'You don't have to be Einstein' equation, his image of himself changed. He was able to 'make the sale' because his beliefs had altered. And by the time his first board meeting came around, Philip was able to give a strong, confident presentation. 'To think I was afraid to go after this job!' he told me later.

We all have conflicts between our aspirations and our apprehensions. Tom Hopkins, in his book *How to Master the Art of Selling*, says, 'Perhaps we can't eliminate this ongoing battle. But we can decide whether we'll lose every day, lose usually, win usually, or win every time. We can't, of course, win every sale . . . That's okay. What isn't okay is to constantly lose out to our same old unresolved fears and anxieties.'

Don't let yourself be ruled by your past. Take the good with you in your search for a new job and leave the bad behind. And there's no point in worrying about whether or not you'll be perfect in the future. If you build your faith on the ability to act in the moment, the future will take care of itself.

BELIEVE IT OR NOT, THE BOSS IS ROOTING FOR YOU

You may not believe this, but most customers *want* a salesperson to be successful. As you'll see in Chapter 26, How to Handle Objections Like a Pro, when a potential buyer says 'but I really can't afford your product', what he really means is, 'please show me the real value of your product so that I can justify spending the money'.

The same principle applies during your job search sales and marketing campaign. The customer, or prospective boss, wants you to make the sale. She *wants* you to be the right person for the job. She wants to end her search. Perhaps she has made a bad decision in employing someone in the past; she certainly doesn't want to repeat that experience. She may have seen a lot of other people and may be beginning to despair that she'll never find the person she needs.

And you think you're nervous!

The interviewer is very often just as nervous as you are and it's an accepted fact that most interviewers don't know how to interview. It's probable that you are (or certainly can become) much better at it than they are.

The interviewer has more at stake than you do. Let's take a look at a prospective boss: Jane, an assistant bank manager in charge of professional development and continuing education. She has had an opening for a new training manager for almost three months, and Jane's boss is impatient for her to recruit someone soon. Other people in the department are complaining about how they are overworked and carrying too much of a load. Jane feels pressured because she couldn't keep the previous employee and because of the complaints from her boss and department personnel. She wants to fill the position quickly, but she still wants to make a good decision. And you think you're nervous!

Look at the job search from the boss's side. You'll be a much better 'salesperson' once you've stood inside your 'client's' shoes.

Jane was hired by the bank because of her abilities and her experience in employee education, not because of her interviewing skills. Like many employers, Jane is not totally clear about what it is she's looking for in a potential employee. Most bosses have a general idea of what they want – someone who's committed, who's a self-starter, responsible, energetic – but they haven't really formulated much of a game plan. Your ability to remain calm, appear confident and ask pertinent questions to obtain information may even help a confused employer get a clearer picture of what she needs. Employers are anxious to employ the right person; the person who will do a great job and make them look good.

The employer also wants to make a good impression on you. After all, if you're an outstanding candidate, you may have several job offers from which to choose, and she wants you to choose hers. Employers suffer from fear of rejection just like interviewees. So go into the interview with empathy and understanding. Reassure the employer that you are the best person for the job. Whatever you can do to reduce the interviewer's anxiety will make it easier for her to say yes to you.

On equal terms

Some salespeople are hesitant about contacting a prospective customer because they feel they might be bothering him or her, or intruding on important work. In my sales seminars I always tell participants to remember that you are there to offer a service to a customer – if you don't have something the customer wants or needs, you shouldn't be there. No salesperson need ever feel inferior or intrusive.

Remember that you and your prospective employer are equals. The fact that you don't have a job and she does means only that and nothing more. Don't ever feel less important because you're looking for a job. You have something of value to offer; that's why you're there. If the interviewer doesn't treat you as an equal, you should have serious doubts about working for her anyway.

Realise that the employer, like the customer, is a person with a problem to be solved and that you are there to solve it. You are there to sell yourself as the person who can anticipate her needs and fill them better than anyone else.

SHIFTING VALUES AND
THE NEW WORK ETHIC

Why do we care about anticipating anyone else's needs? Why do we work at all? I've heard many people say the real reason they work is to make a lot of money. Yet if you describe a job that really doesn't interest them, those same people will say, 'You couldn't pay me enough to do that job!' Your job search marketing efforts should reflect your personal goals and reasons for working.

The goals we set for ourselves include more than status symbols and financial success. In the 90s we're not only re-examining how, when and where we work; we're also looking at why.

A few years ago I ran into my neighbour, George, loading several boxes into the lift of our building. George had been an accountant with the same large firm for over 12 years, and often complained loudly about his job. I asked George how things were going at work.

'I hate work,' he said. 'I guess I'm just basically lazy. I don't want to get up in the morning. I work with numbers all day, I come home and collapse in front of the TV. Work is just boring. But it pays fairly well – enough for me to have bought myself a present,' he said, pointing to the boxes on the floor beside him. They contained an elaborate stereo system and he started to tell me about its amazing features. I asked him who was going to put the system together for him.

'Oh, I am,' he said, and his eyes began to sparkle, his voice became animated and his whole body came alive as he described how carefully he'd chosen each of the components and how he couldn't wait to get started putting the complicated system together. It would take him hours, he said.

'Sounds like a lot of work,' I said.

'What do you mean?' he asked. 'Just think what I get when I'm done: a terrific sound system like I always wanted, not to mention the pride and sense of accomplishment knowing I did it myself. Work? That's not work!'

Does George remind you of anyone you know? Do you ever feel the way he does about getting up in the morning? Just what does work mean to you? Is it something you look forward to? Or do you start off every week with the 'Monday morning blues'? Are you dissatisfied with your present job?

Although most people spend more than 96,000 hours of their lives working, only a minority derive satisfaction and excitement from their work. The average person is resigned to the idea of having to work, and looks forward to retirement to do what he or she wants. People look for satisfaction and fulfilment *outside* the workplace; there's a sharp division between work and non-work.

Employers are also realising that people who are excited by and about their work are more productive, more creative and more dedicated employees. I asked Robert Blinder, Senior V.P. Director of Corporate Resources at Prudential-Bache what he looks for in his employees. 'I look for intelligent, hard-working, knowledgeable people,' he said. 'People who like what they do so much that they'll be happy spending a lot of time doing it.'

We're less willing to spend 96,000 unhappy hours working in order to have 'a life' at some later time – we're willing to work hard now, as long as we can also have the quality of life we desire.

My neighbour George found this out. The large company he worked for was bought out by an even larger one, and George was offered early retirement. He accepted a generous settlement and joined a small electronics repair service, specialising in stereo systems, TVs and VCRs. The business is doing very well, and George has a new attitude about work. Now when I run into him he tells me he is 'exhausted, but happy'. He took the *knowledge that he already had* – even though it was something he had always considered a hobby – and *took positive actions* to make his work a more integral and satisfying part of his life. This is the new work ethic.

More of ourselves

What do we get out of this new work ethic? Optimistic as it may sound, what we get is much more *of* ourselves and *for* ourselves.

It has been proven that job stress can lead to burn-out, illness, and the destruction of personal relationships. As a society we have measured success in terms of money, power and title. Many 'successful' people are neither happy nor satisfied, however. Yuppies who work 70 hours a week for the money and the status get burned out very quickly because their relationship is between money and self-worth, not work and self-worth.

In the industrial age, our parents and grandparents worked long, hard hours at uninteresting or unrewarding jobs. They had little independence or responsibility. They went to work, got their wage packets and came home. There are still people like that, people who like to have everything laid out and controlled for them. However, if you're interested in becoming a happier, more productive and better paid member of the workforce, then I am speaking to you. The new work ethic provides you with the crucial ingredients to form a positive relationship *between your work and your sense of self-worth*.

TAKE A POSITIVE ATTITUDE

We have explored several important themes in this chapter:

To sell yourself you have to believe in yourself. Have confidence in yourself and others will have confidence in you. You can't stand out from the crowd until you can stand up for yourself. Rejection is a normal part of the job search process, not a personal indictment. Learning to learn from your mistakes and experiences is an important part of the selling process.

Success is attained by setting goals and following through. Sometimes we're afraid to set important goals because they appear distant and unreachable. Don't think of yourself as starting from Point A and magically arriving at Point B; instead envisage yourself going through each step, learning from any possible mistakes, and, most of all, *enjoying the process*.

When your work is more valuable to you, you're more valuable to your work. The new work ethic tells us to look for work that adds to our sense of self worth. Positive input and effort into our work produces better quality goods and services. When work becomes more than just a fast buck, it's a true expression of how we value our time and energy.

You'll never be 'selling out' if you follow your true instincts and have faith in your dreams. Selling yourself to others only proves that you have confidence in yourself and are willing to stand behind your beliefs. When you don't believe in yourself, you're only selling yourself short.

The next section of this book deals with 'Success Factors,' those skills and personal characteristics that will enable you to succeed in any job or career. The more of these you have to offer, the easier it will be to market yourself and the more valuable you will be.

But before you go on, take a few moments to consider your present situation. What is your work ethic like now? What steps can you take right now to improve your attitude, use the knowledge you have now, and take positive action?

PART TWO

THE SUCCESS FACTORS:
Your Ten Most Marketable Skills

4

SUCCESS FACTOR 1:
Adaptability

'An effective marketer isn't resistant to change, but views it as a challenge and an opportunity'

P erhaps the most important personal quality necessary for success today is adaptability: the ability to adjust yourself easily and willingly to changing conditions. Your attitude towards change can make the difference between getting ahead and standing still.

If you see change as a challenge and a chance to prove yourself, your value to a potential employer will increase. Susan Boren, Vice President of Human Resources of Dayton Hudson Corporation has this to say about adaptability: 'Personal adaptability is vital to us. As business changes we need employees who can change also. And they must view change as an opportunity.'

ADAPTABILITY SPELLS SUCCESS

Change as opportunity could be the secret to success in the years ahead. Myra and Joan are both rising young executives in XYZ Corporation. They have both received memos stating that management is installing a new computer system which everyone will be expected to learn so that important data can be accessed whenever needed.

Myra is thrilled at the prospect. She has been annoyed at having to wait for someone else to bring her information she needed, and now she will be able to obtain it herself. She sees this not only as a way to be more productive, but also as an opportunity to learn a new skill.

Joan, however, thinks, 'I'll never have time to learn this system and I'll probably never use it anyway. If I need some data, I'll just have someone bring me the information I need.' She spends several sleepless nights worrying and calls in sick on the day of the installation. When a promotion opportunity arises, Joan can't understand why Myra is chosen over her as she has put in more hours than Myra and produced all of her work on time.

I see this scenario over and over again as new systems and technologies are introduced. Joan would recieve a low rating in this important Success Factor of adaptability. She is inflexible. She has a narrow vision of the future. Are you more like Joan or Myra? Are you easily upset by anything that seems to threaten the status quo?

Some careers demand more flexibility than others, of course. Accountants, for example, who will be in great demand over the next few years, often see several different clients during a given week. They usually set up in a make-shift or borrowed work area. My accountant, Beth, also works for a petrol station where she usually has to share a table with auto parts and cans of motor oil. The next client she visits may set her up in the chairman's office or in a corner of the post room. She had to learn to adapt her way of working to the change of clients and physical surroundings.

CONQUERING THE UNKNOWN

We all have our own ways of working, ways that give us comfort and security. When presented with an unexpected problem, we tend to react according to our usual patterns. Why is it often so difficult to break out of these patterns? It usually has to do with *fear of the unknown*. The way we know, works. Who knows what will happen if we try another way? We imagine all kinds of tragic and humiliating consequences. The reality is that although the results may not be exactly what we had in mind they are rarely tragic or humiliating. Once you begin to make a fairer assessment of a particular set of circumstances, you can begin to change your habitual reactions and take the appropriate new action.

When you encounter a problem, ask yourself the following questions:

- How is this situation unique?
- What's the best way to handle this particular situation (or person)?
- What is my usual mode of dealing with problems?
- What works?
- What doesn't?
- When was the last time I handled something in a new way?
- In terms of my bottom-line objective, how would I like this situation to turn out?
- How can I get out of my own way and make that happen?

If you are by nature overly resistant to change, it's important to analyse your behaviour when change is introduced. Learn to recognise your resistance and ask yourself why it's so important that you hold on to your way of doing things. There's no need to jump on every passing bandwagon, but you should be able to weigh the old against the new in a spirit of open-mindedness.

Adaptability can benefit you as much as your company. Suppose that you unexpectedly lose your job. If you are an adaptable person, your ego may be bruised but you'll be able to learn from your experience, evaluate your skills, create a marketing plan, and go on to a better opportunity. You'll have a practical strategy and will feel good about your ability to move on. And if you feel good about yourself, you won't be devastated by unforeseen changes in your life.

TURNING YOUR FEARS AROUND

Can you turn your fears around and make change work for you? Find out by answering True or False to each of the numbered statements.

When you contemplate making changes in your work or personal life, you:

1. Think you have to give up everything you know and start again.
2. Feel that you're being forced to do things you don't want to do.
3. See yourself as a creature of habit, and believe that you can't teach an old dog new tricks.
4. Think if you try something new, you might make a mistake.
5. Think that change involves pain and hard work.

If you said 'True' to any of the statements then you are probably resistant to change, and would benefit from some work on changing your attitude. Here are some helpful hints to combat the five myths:

1. *You think you have to give up everything you know and start all over again.* Not true. When you adapt one thing to another, you take what is usable from the first and apply it to the second. No need to reinvent the wheel. Concentrate on developing transferable skills-like the ten Success Factors.

2. *You feel that you are being forced to do things you don't want to do.* If you're always waiting for 'the other shoe to drop,' it will. Which do you think is a more painful experience: being evicted from an apartment you can't afford, or choosing to look for a smaller, less expensive space? Or altering your entire lifestyle after you've had a heart attack, or starting a moderate programme of good food and exercise when you're still perfectly healthy?

It's always more difficult to make changes when they're imposed on us by outside sources. Think of change as a catalyst for improving your life, not as a hardship forced on your by circumstance.

3. *You see yourself as a creature of habit, and you believe that you can't teach an old dog new tricks.* Hugh was always extremely predictable. Others in his office said, 'You can set your clock by Hugh.' They often did. He arrived every morning at five to nine, had the same black coffee and cherry danish, ate it in exactly five minutes, and promptly began his day. He left for lunch on the dot of twelve and returned at one o'clock precisely. He stopped work exactly at five.

Hugh was 49 when the company was bought out by a larger firm. They wanted to promote Hugh but Hugh didn't want a new position. He felt he was good at the job he had, so why change? But the rest of the company changed around him, and eventually Hugh had to face an even bigger change – his job was phased out, and he was forced to leave.

Rapid changes are overtaking businesses all over the country. Employers are looking for people who can handle change with ease and enthusiasm. When it comes to developing your adaptability, don't think about changing old habits – think about forming new ones. Make it a habit to try one new thing every day. Take a different route home from school or into work or back from dropping off the kids at day care. Read a book about a subject you've never heard of. Small changes sometimes bring big surprises. And before you know it, you'll be looking foward to the 'change of the day'.

4. *You think if you try something new, you might make a mistake.* Well, you might. Everybody makes mistakes. We learn to learn from our mistakes, to analyse what went wrong and go on from there. Corny as it may sound, those who are successful in coping with change learn to pick themselves up, dust themselves off and start all over again.

5. *You think that change involves pain and hard work.* It might. It depends on your attitude. It may be difficult for you to accept some of the ideas and suggestions I make in this book. But the big question is this: Are you unhappy? Because if you are, then how much is your happiness worth? Is it worth some temporary discomfort as you go through a transition period? Is the result worth the effort? That's one you'll have to answer yourself.

Before going onto Chapter 5, make a list of the positive actions you can take today to improve your adaptability skills.

5

SUCCESS FACTOR 2:
Commitment

'With so many similar products and services today competing for the same markets, the commitment of the salesperson is often the deciding factor'

I PLEDGE ALLEGIANCE TO MYSELF

The subject of loyalty and commitment comes up often in my management seminars. One manager expressed to me the feelings of most top executives: 'I'd rather have a hard-working, committed person who stays with the company for two years than an unmotivated, complacent employee who's around for the long haul. As a matter of fact, we'll go out of our way to accommodate a valuable employee in terms of scheduling problems or other individual needs. We just need those kind of people around.'

Our definition of commitment on the job is changing as we move into a new century and different ways of working. Arthur Denny Scott of Goldman, Sachs and Co., sees the diminishment of corporate loyalty as the way of the future. Scott, who worked for IBM for 28 years, says 'More and more, loyalties are toward personal interest, to a profession or a career. Engineers may remain engineers, for example, but move around from one place to another. Going to work for IBM used to be like a marriage, and that kind of relationship will no longer exist.'

As we move from the era of 'corporate marriage' into the 'divorce age', companies and employees are becoming less willing or able to make such long-term commitments. Years ago, when you joined XYZ Corporation, XYZ expected a long-term (perhaps lifetime) commitment from you, and you expected long-term support (financial and otherwise) from the company. Changing technologies, as well as the trend towards buy-outs, mergers and take-overs make long-term commitments very rare.

But just because long-term commitment is changing, that doesn't mean there is no commitment at all. It means that, although we may not be able to promise we'll stay with a particular company for the next 20 years, we must be *committed to doing the task at hand*, and giving it our best. The emphasis is changing from quantity to quality.

GOOD HABITS START EARLY

Commitment is a habit that can be developed at any stage. If you are still in school, your commitment can be to your schoolwork or to the after-school job you have (even if it's for little or no wages). My neighbour's son, Howard, worked at many summer and after-school jobs throughout high school and college and received several offers for full-time employment from these companies after graduation. Why? Because he's committed to doing well at whatever he's doing, and employers translate this as a willingness to work hard and a concern for the company's benefit as well as his own.

Companies both large and small appreciate that attitude. In my own organisation, I had a part-time employee, Lisa, who had to go out of town for a few weeks. She was so concerned that she arranged for her own replacement, brought him in the week before she left and trained him herself. Needless to say, this extra effort was greatly appreciated and told me a lot about Lisa's 'success factors'.

Large companies also appreciate this sense of commitment. One of the changes we're seeing in today's workforce is the increased use of temporary workers; one of the reasons temps are becoming so popular is that many of the temporary workers are very committed to doing a good job, whether they're at a place for a day, a week, or a month. Most people who work as temps do so because it fits their current needs and lifestyle. They know that the agency will use them often if they're reliable and perform well on each assignment.

Take Allen for example. Allen was a temp worker for a large publishing concern; the company had a policy that they never hired part-time employees on a permanent basis. Allen was a very hard worker, committed to doing a good job while he was there. He even made several suggestions for improving procedures for other temporary employees. The company wanted to hire Allen full time, but he was going to college at the time, and couldn't take a full time position. Yet, because of Allen's commitment to produce quality work the company eventually took him on permanently, something he was repeatedly told could never happen. Allen became a valuable asset to his department.

When he finished school and looked back over his accomplishments, Allen found many other events in his life that demonstrated a high level of commitment. Discovering he had this valuable, marketable skill gave Allen extra confidence and was a strong selling point for potential employers.

Every industry has been affected by changes in definitions of loyalty and commitment. According to Dr Richard E. Emmert, Executive Director of the American Institute of Chemical Engineers, 'People are changing jobs several times through the course of a career; companies are less paternalistic, employees less loyal. There are more people working through service firms and as independent contractors rather than directly for the company needing the service.'

In the future, many companies will consist of a large network of freelancers and consultants, individuals and small groups of people who are working independently towards a common goal. Whether you do this within a corporate structure or actually go out on your own into business for yourself, your survival will depend on your commitment to doing the work.

INVEST IN YOUR COMMITMENT

What is your commitment to work? Think about how your atittude affects your performance. What can you do to improve your current situation? Try to see how committing yourself to your work will pay dividends down the road. If you can't make a commitment to what you're presently doing, it may be time for a change.

Look at your present responsibilities at home, at school, or on the job:

- Do you go about them half- or whole-heartedly?
- How would your boss, your parents or your teacher answer that question?
- When was the last time you really extended yourself?
- How did it make you feel when you did?

Even if no one else recognises the difference in your attitude, it will make a difference to you.

Do you have problems making commitments? Break down your resistance into manageable chunks. It's possible to do something for one hour or one day that may seem impossible to do forever. You can honestly make a pledge to do your best and have the discipline to do what is needed for the immediate situation, one task at a time. It's necessary to have goals and make plans for the future, but no one says you have to accomplish them all at once.

THE HONOUR SYSTEM AT WORK

Reliability and responsibility are important requirements for today's employees. You must keep the promises you make to yourself as well as to others. People don't expect you to be perfect, but they do expect you to be there on time and to be focused. If you're disorganised and scatty, try breaking your time down into manageable pieces so that tasks do not become overwhelming. Keep a diary or note book with you always, and jot down ideas the moment they occur so that you won't forget anything. Take a reality check every once in a while to make sure you haven't made promises you can't keep or taken on too many projects at once.

Reliability

Steve, a college classmate of mine, was bright, industrious and creative. He would consistently turn in interesting and original term papers – two weeks late. His enthusiasm for a new sport or hobby was extreme and catching. He would get all of his friends involved, then his interest would shift and he would leave his team mates wondering what had happened to their staunchest supporter.

Steve came top of the class every term. In his second year, he managed to get interviews with five of the country's top law firms for summer internship programmes – then was late for three of the appointments, went to the wrong address for the fourth and forgot about the fifth one altogether. He is now a moderately successful lawyer, never having risen to his full potential because he is not reliable.

Responsibility

Work in this country is now heading into its most exciting and challenging stage: companies are beginning to treat their employees as adults, to trust and respect their individual talents and abilities. Walter F. Whitt, V.P. Corporate Human Resources Services at McGraw-Hill, says that '. . . corporations are beginning to permit employees to be more autonomous, to be more accountable and to have a broader range of responsibilities. There's less emphasis on rote-type "good work" and a lot more on thinking and decision-making capabilities.'

The new ideal for the corporate structure is to have ideas generated at all levels and rising to the top like a balloon – with management choosing the best of these as solutions. This will replace the 'trickle down' style, where a single solution to a problem, good or bad, was made by top management and issued on down the line.

Susan Boren, Vice President Human Resources Dayton Hudson Corporation feels that her company is '. . . placing more and more value on real communication with our employees. Hudson's was for a long time a family business, and we felt we had to "take care" of our workers. We still care about our employees, but now they're more our partners than our children. We listen to their ideas and treat them with more respect, as adults who must take care of themselves.'

Just as it is in the family situation, this trust and respect is not given unconditionally or indiscriminately. It is given only to those who earn it.

Corporations that have traditionally given responsibility only to senior executives are realising that in order to provide service to their customers, the responsibility and authority to make decisions must be decentralised. Susan Boren sees Dayton Hudson continuing to embrace this philosophy: 'In the next 20 years, we will be continuing to empower people at lower levels, to provide them with enough information for them to make good decisions in order to provide better service.'

NOT 'WHY ME?' BUT 'WHAT NOW?'

The 'company man' of the industrial age, who conformed with every company rule and did exactly what he was told and no more, wasn't willing to take any responsibility for himself or his actions. Adaptable, creative, independent people are willing to take more risks – and live with the consequences.

Do you have a 'why me?' attitude? Do you think you're unlucky and that bad things just happen to you? If so, you'll need a change of attitude to succeed in the future. Instead of focusing on 'why', starting thinking about 'what'. Don't think 'Why do I always act this way?', but rather 'What can I do differently this time?'

Janet heard a rumour in her medical lab that her particular field of research was being discontinued. She'd been working at this lab for eight years, and she had accepted orders from her supervisors and never said a word. She had been passed over for promotion, but didn't complain because she wasn't sure if she could handle managing the six others in her department.

Janet began to discuss the situation with Marie, a co-worker for the past four years. 'Aren't you worried?' she asked Marie. 'I hear they're shutting us down altogether, and you know there's no other work like this around. I don't know what I'll do if I lose my job. Why is this happening to me?'

'I was worried at first,' Marie replied. 'But then I went up to the front office to talk. I'd heard that they're refitting this lab for high tech equipment for AIDS research. I've been interested in that field anyway, and I asked them what I'd have to do to be part of the new team. They told me they would let me train at one of the other labs up north where they're already using the new equipment. Then when they open the new lab down here, they'll transfer me back.'

Marie was willing to take a chance and talk to her boss. She let the company know she was willing to learn new things; accept a new challenge. She was willing to take responsibility for her own life – not just to react to events, but to act upon them.

In fields such as medical research and health care services, responsibility is a more necessary quality than ever before. These are fast growing career areas, and candidates with a background that shows a strong sense of responsibility will be sought after and pursued.

Before going on to Chapter 6 make a list of the positive actions you can take today to improve your commitment skills.

6

SUCCESS FACTOR 3:
Communications

'Increase your selling power by improving your communications: be sure that your message is received the way that you sent it and meant it'

R elating to other people is the basic function of communications skills, and in the age of the service society, working well with other people will be the best way to achieve success. And working well with other people is 100 per cent communications. Can you even imagine a job done in total isolation?

How we communicate with the people we work with is as important as the work itself. 'You can have the personality of a tree stump and work on an assembly line,' says Arthur Denny Scott of Goldman Sachs. 'But in a service society personal relations become much more important. If you've only valued physical skills, you'll be in deep trouble. You must be able to project yourself into the mind-set of the other person and see things from his perspective.'

If you send a potential employer a letter filled with grammatical errors and spelling mistakes you surely won't get a positive response. If you go into an interview and introduce yourself with a flimsy handshake, then sit on the edge of your chair nervously cracking your knuckles, your qualifications and past experience will be of very little value to you.

If, however, you are well-spoken, project confidence and write sharply a certain lack of experience might be overlooked.

It often happens in a job search scenario that your initial contact with a potential employer is your marketing letter (see Chapter 23). Expressing yourself clearly, concisely and correctly will create a powerful first impressive – and make you a serious contender for any job. Put yourself in an employer's position. What if you received a typed letter that began:

Dear Sir

I am lloking for a job as a secrtrary. Do you need won?

I doubt you would read any further. You certainly wouldn't care about the letter writer's previous experience, and you would have to question how motivated they would be on the job if they can't take the time to proof read an introductory letter.

In this case, it's not the 'thought that counts'. People notice even small mistakes, so putting that extra effort into written communications is well worth the time.

Practice, as always, makes perfect, so keep writing and rewriting until you are satisfied that there are no errors. Use a dictionary, a thesaurus, and guides to style and grammar. An original idea is no good to anyone if you're the only one who can understand what you've written.

Oral communications are equally important. How many times have you made judgments about people based on nothing more than the way they sound over the telephone? It's not necessary to become a public speaker to succeed in business, but having a good strong voice inspires trust and implies confidence and competence.

THE PRINCIPLES OF
PERSUASIVE COMMUNICATIONS

Everyone in business today is, in effect, a salesperson. Whether you're selling yourself to your current boss, a potential boss, clients, or customers, the basics of selling remain the same. The best salespeople are those who use persuasive communications to help the buyer discover the connection between their needs and the product the salesperson is offering. This is as important in selling yourself as it is in selling any product. Here are the four basic principles of persuasive communications:

1. We communicate in many different ways

What you say is, of course, important, but so is *how* you say it. Your tone of voice says a lot about you.

When I was looking for a part-time assistant for my office, I did a lot of preliminary interviewing over the phone. Since the person I was looking for would be required to answer the phone, voice quality was a critical factor in my decision. The first day two women called. They both seemed very nice, and intelligent and could easily handle the tasks I had in mind for this position. But the second woman who called had very little energy in her voice. I had to ask her to speak up twice. I liked what she had to say, and I'm sure she could have done the job, but I couldn't give it to her because of the quality of her voice.

We also communicate through body language. Do you have a nervous habit that you always carry with you? Do you bite your nails or twist your fingers into knots? Do you have good posture or do you slouch over, head down and shoulders forward?

Millions of pounds are spent every year by marketing experts on design and packaging. They know that the way a product is presented has a lot to do with how it is accepted. The same goes for you. When you go in to sell your services to a potential employer, are you aware of the impression you are making, physically and verbally.

If you walk into an interview with uncombed hair, a slouch and a shuffle, you'll have to work very hard to get the employer to see beyond the 'packaging.' Ask your friends or family for feedback about how you present yourself, and how they perceive your body language and posture.

2. People respond from their point of view, based on past experience

Languages develop differently in different parts of the world because of each culture's unique circumstances. The Eskimos, for example, have over 100 words meaning snow. There is one that means snow that is for drinking water, one for snow spread out over the land, another for snow that has just fallen, and 97 more for other types of snow. Snow is of primary importance in Eskimos' lives, and their language reflects that.

All communication depends on your point of view.

Words mean different things to different people. Here is a list of words that may have strong emotional impact. Write down your feelings about each word:
Criminal
Lawyer
Boss
Television
Work
Religion
Money
Now ask two other people to do the same thing. You will find the three sets of responses are very different from one another.

Effective selling requires effective communication, so be sure that you are communicating in the way you intend. If you describe yourself as a workaholic, for instance, one potential boss may see that as a positive trait, while another may see it as negative. Be sure to express yourself clearly and precisely and ask a potential employer to clarify anything he says that seems ambiguous to you.

3. People respond according to their needs not yours

This is an essential rule of successful selling. When you go to buy a car, you go because you want or need a new car – not because the salesperson wants to sell it to you. If you don't want that car, it's going to be a very difficult sale.

If you ask your boss for a raise, you'll get it because your boss needs you – not because you need the extra money. And if you are offered a job its because the company needs you and you can fill it's needs, not because you need employment. You won't sell yourself by saying, 'Employ me. I need a job.' You will sell yourself by saying, 'Employ me. I can help you solve your problem.'

4. The only way to find out where people are coming from and what their needs are is through a planned process of questioning and active listening

Asking the right questions and knowing how to listen are two of the most effective communications tools.

Asking the right question will get you the information you need when you need it. People love to answer questions – they feel compelled to answer them. People automatically pay more attention to a question than they do to a statement. Even the shyest person will respond to a question directed at him; ask the right question and you'll wonder why you ever thought he was shy!

Knowing how to listen will allow you to receive information as it's intended to be communicated. Epictitus, the Greek philosopher, once said, 'God has wisely given us two ears and one mouth so we may hear twice as much as we speak.'

THE LISTENING QUIZ

Here is a simple quiz to help you improve your listening skills:

	Usually	Sometimes	Seldom

When talking to people, do you:
1. Prepare yourself physically by facing the speaker, and making sure you can hear.   _____   _____   _____

2. Watch the speaker as well as listen to him.   _____   _____   _____

45

	Usually	Sometimes	Seldom
3. Decide from the speaker's appearance and delivery whether or not what he has to say is worthwhile.	_____	_____	_____
4. Listen primarily for ideas and underlying feelings.	_____	_____	_____
5. Determine your own bias, if any, and try to allow for it?	_____	_____	_____
6. Keep your mind on what the speaker is saying.	_____	_____	_____
7. Interrupt immediately if you hear a statement you feel is wrong.	_____	_____	_____
8. Make sure before answering that you've taken in the other person's point of view.	_____	_____	_____
9. Try to have the last word.	_____	_____	_____
10. Make a conscious effort to evaluate the logic and credibility of what you hear.	_____	_____	_____

Score: Questions 1, 2, 4, 5, 6, 8, 10: 10 points for 'usually', 5 for 'sometimes', 0 for 'seldom'.

Questions 3, 7, 9: no points for 'usually', 5 points for 'sometimes', 10 points for 'seldom'.

If your score is below 70, you have developed some bad listening habits; if it is 70–85, you listen well but could improve; if it is 90 or above, you are an excellent listener.

COMMUNICATION IS THE WORD

Communications covers a wide area, but the basic skill involves getting your thoughts or ideas across to another party – on a one-to-one personal basis, to 10 or 12 people across a board room table, or to millions of viewers across a TV screen. The way you communicate says a lot about you; especially when you are in the process of marketing yourself. We communicate in obvious ways and ways that are not so obvious; all of these ways can be studied, practised and mastered.

Before going on to the next chapter make a list of the positive actions you can take today to improve your communications skills.

7

SUCCESS FACTOR 4:
Creativity

'Selling is creative problem solving: how best to get what you
want while giving the customer what he or she needs'

H ow do you view creativity? Just because you're not a Picasso or a
Hemingway doesn't mean you're not creative. Creativity is really
about different ways of looking at things. Picasso had a particular vision
of the world and expressed it through his art; Hemingway expressed his
vision through the written word; Beethoven and Bruce Springsteen used
music to share their views. Albert Einstein and Madame Curie expressed
their creativity in scientific terms. Luckily for the rest of us, all creativity
does not require genius. It begins with taking an objective look at a problem or an obstacle, and combining imagination and reason to discover a
solution.

A friend, an office manager in a small dental clinic, once said to me, 'I
don't see myself as a very creative person.' Yet I've always admired her
ingenuity and resourcefulness. Faced with seemingly insurmountable
difficulties, she always manages to find an effective solution. She was surprised when I told her I thought this showed great creative talent.

Most people don't think they're creative at work. As a consultant,
when I ask most managers what they do, they tell me they plan, control,
organise staff and lead. When I ask them if their job is creative, they say
no. But a manager's main job is to deal with problems, and creativity
applies to every kind of problem that exists. Every time you find a new
way to work something out, you're being creative, manager or not.

It doesn't take much creative thinking for a job on an assembly line.
But as we develop into more and more of a service society, the need for
creativity in the workplace increases. Walter F. Whitt, Vice President of
Corporate Human Resources at McGraw Hill, sees management becoming

more creative, 'more entrepreneurial, more willing to take calculated risks – people who are not constrained by narrow vision and who are able to think conceptually'.

A QUIZ TO DEVELOP YOUR CREATIVE FLOW

This quiz is intended to give you an idea of how you view yourself and your own creativity. The 25 questions can help you develop the flow of creative ideas. There are no right or wrong answers.

1. Do you enjoy 'the creative process' – experimenting with new ideas or new ways to do things?

2. Do you accept things as they are because you think 'it's always been done this way'?

3. Do you believe that following the rules is more important than getting the job done, or are you willing to bend them a little?

4. What do you do when you don't like something, or you have to wait too long, or you see time or materials being wasted? Do you complain? Or do you look for ways to fix it?

5. Are you naturally curious?

6. When you see something that is particularly useful or ingenious, do you think of ways you can adapt it for use in your own job or personal life?

7. When faced with a problem, do you stick at it until it's solved?

8. Do you consider many different options before taking action?

9. What was the last good idea you had? What made it a good idea? How did it come to you?

10. Do you ever just sit and daydream, or doodle on a piece of paper? Do you enjoy it, or do you feel you're wasting time?

11. Are you judgmental about your efforts before you even finish a project?

12. Do you get frustrated with yourself if you can't solve a problem immediately? Or do you give yourself a chance to come up with a better solution?

13. Have you found any new and interesting ways to stimulate your creativity, such as walking in the woods, taking a bubble bath or meditating?

14. Do you read in your spare time? If so what do you read?

15. Are you familiar with resource materials and facilities? Do you know where the library is? The local college? Do you read trade journals or business publications?

16. Do you enjoy playing games?

17. What do you think about the job you do? Do you see creative opportunities in your work?

18. Are you open to new ideas and suggestions from others – no matter who they may be?

19. Are you supportive of someone else who comes up with a good idea?

20. What's your biggest problem at work at the moment?

21. Have you tried breaking it down into smaller, more manageable challenges?

22. Do you know anyone else who's had a similar problem and may be able to help you out?

23. Do you tend to think that creativity is reserved for artists and doesn't apply to you?

24. What do you do when a problem has you stumped? Do you give up easily?

25. Do you ever see solving a problem as fun?

LOOKING AT PROBLEMS FROM ANOTHER ANGLE

The next time you're faced with a problem to solve, try and look at it as an exercise in creativity. Step back and analyse it objectively without being judgmental. Ask yourself, 'What is *interesting* about this problem?' Look at it from that angle, and see what solutions evolve. Then try another angle. Then try the angle that struck you immediately, the one you decided against because it seemed too simple, or too difficult, or even ridiculous.

Don't worry about the details, or try to figure out how much it will cost. Just consider the overall picture and look for a broad conceptual approach. Don't reject any possibility just because it's flawed. Creativity involves the ability to go beyond routine solutions to come up with a new idea or a new application of an old one.

Creative people don't get locked into a single path. When change comes they can find ways to make it work for them. They find new applications for old technologies, which, in these times, is the only way companies are going to be able to survive.

The more creative you are, the more valuable you will be to any organisation. On the job, consider any problem as an invitation to flex your creative muscles. You – and your employer – just might be pleasantly surprised.

Before going on to the next chapter make a list of the positive actions you can take today to improve your creative skills.

8
SUCCESS FACTOR 5:
Decision-making

'Marketing often requires quick and confident decisions.
That doesn't mean you have to be right all the time – we
learn from all our choices'

Think of how many decisions you make in the course of a day. Some of us are very good at it, and make decisions with ease and assurance. Many of us do not. Our ability to make decisions has to do with our willingness to trust ourselves and our own judgments.

The more decisions you make, the better you get at it. Living with constant change and uncertainty the need for strong decision-making abilities is greater than ever. Aven Kerr, V.P. of Human Resource at The Prudential, says that decision-making is a highly valued skill because '. . . everything about business is happening faster and faster. Information comes flooding in and there just isn't as much time to make a decision as there used to be.'

Your market value will increase in direct proportion to your decision-making abilities.

THE 'DECIDING' FORMULA:
RESEARCH, ANALYSIS AND TRUST

Jason was in a period he called 'between lifestyles'. He had been working as a photographer's assistant for several years, thinking he would one day set up on his own. Discouraged, he felt that he was not moving along fast enough and that photography was no longer his main interest. He wanted to get married and start raising a family (and his fiancée wanted to be an at-home mother), but he was not very confident that he could support a family on an assistant's salary. Jason decided to switch careers.

A friend offered him a job as a jewellery salesman. Jason accepted the offer and spent the next year and a half trying to convince himself that he had made the right decision, even though the job made him increasingly unhappy. He felt obligated to his friend, and was afraid of making another wrong move. Finally he realised that he missed being around photography. This time Jason was much more careful in his decision-making process. He made a list of all the things he enjoyed most about photography, as well the reasons he had left it. Then he listed those things he liked and disliked about selling jewellery.

He discovered he had learned a great deal about selling but not very much about jewellery (he had no real interest in it). He was, however, deeply interested in cameras. He put salesmanship and cameras together and is now one of the most knowledgeable photographic equipment salesmen in the business. And he loves his work.

Jason's original decision to change jobs was made hastily and emotionally. His second decision was well thought out, based upon analysis of the facts, study of future options, and trust in his decision-making abilities.

NINE STEPS TO MAKING A GOOD DECISION

Making a good decision involves taking risks. You can never be sure of the outcome, but you can make the best decision possible at the present time. There are nine steps to making a good decision:

1. Pinpoint the decision that needs to be made. Make sure you define the problem so that it can be broken down into specific issues that determine the final decision.

2. Try to get as much information as possible. Realise, however, that you can't get *all* the information there is; at some point you will just have to make do with what you have.

3. Make sure your information is reliable. Check facts and figures yourself whenever possible.

4. Ask for suggestions and advice. You don't have to follow it, but you may find out some things you didn't know before.

5. Make plus and minus columns (or pros and cons), and see which side tips the scale. When Benjamin Franklin had a problem to solve or a decision to make, he would take out a piece of paper and draw a line down the middle of it. To the left of the line he would write 'Yes' and to the right of the line he would put the word 'No'. In the 'Yes' column, Ben Franklin would list all the reasons to take a given action. In the 'No' column, he would list all the reasons not to. Then he would go with whichever list was longer. His decision was made for him.

6. *Ask yourself what would be the best possible outcome of this decision?* And what would be the worst? What is most likely to happen? What will happen if you don't do it?

7. *List all possible solutions to your problem and their likely consequences* (just remember you can never be absolutely sure of the consequences). Then determine the value of each solution and its consequence. List the good and bad points of each one; then compare them all to find the best solution in its proper perspective. Ask yourself 'If I make this decision, where will I be in six months from now? In a year? In five years?'

8. *Trust your intuition.* Ask yourself why this feels right or feels wrong. Learn to trust your deeper instincts instead of following your immediate impulse.

9. *Recognise errors and use them to improve your decision-making skills for the next time.* When Jason originally chose to change careers, he made an emotional, hasty decision that led him to a job he was not well-suited to. But the year and a half he spent in the jewellery business was not at all wasted. Jason discovered he could sell, and he used his time to learn more and more about the art of salesmanship. All his experience in the jewellery business led him to the work he now loves.

Before going onto the next chapter make a list of the positive actions you can take today to improve your decision-making skills?

9

SUCCESS FACTOR 6:
Evaluation

'The best sales question you can ask yourself is, "How can I do it better next time?"'

MAKING GOOD JUDGMENTS

If you were alone in the office working under a tight deadline and the computer went down, what would you do? Would you tell yourself there's nothing you can do about it? Would you panic, give in to fears that you'd lose your job, and start to cry? Or would you be able to look at the work load, set priorities, and find ways to solve the most immediate problems?

Obviously, employers are looking for people who fit into the last category. Your ability to make reasonable judgments and assess unexpected situations is of great value on any job. This is the skill of evaluation, and it's one you use over and over again – in every area of your life.

A simple act like crossing the street requires an evaluation of the risks involved. Is a car coming? How fast is it going? Can you make it safely to the other side? First you evaluate the risks, then you make your decision. You use evaluation skills every time you make a purchase, and every time you make a new acquaintance.

At work, the same kinds of evaluation skills are needed. You may be asked to evaluate situations (such as the computer failure mentioned above), purchases (anything from office supplies to company mergers), and people (co-workers, staff and supervisors).

MAKING BETTER JUDGMENTS

The evaluations you make in every day life are often hastily formed subjective opinions and gut feelings. Making an evaluation at work, however, requires more than a gut feeling. It requires an *objective* opinion, based on a set of formal standards. Most people rely on surface impressions and instinct. A good evaluator listens to instinct, but doesn't rely on it.

Formal evaluation is a three-step process:

1. Describe the object of your evaluation. Is it a person, place or situation? Is it the job someone is performing? Is it a purchase to be made?

2. Set up a list of standards. Suppose you're in charge of finding a new pencil supplier for your office. What standards will the supplier have to meet for you to make a positive decision? Your list might include:

- Top quality
- Low cost
- Ability to deliver large quantities
- Ability to deliver within a week of receiving the order
- Ability to imprint company name on pencils
- Pencils must have good quality erasers

3. Compare the object of your evaluation to the list of standards. You've found four pencil suppliers. If only one meets all six of the standards you set up, you will choose that supplier. If two suppliers meet your criteria, you will set up more standards to make an evaluation between them.

These three steps apply to any kind of evaluation you're making. This process can be used to make a one-time decision (such as choosing a supplier), or as an on-going process (such as assessing the performance level of your staff).

PERFORMANCE APPRAISAL: A GOOD AND FAIR ASSESSMENT

Performance appraisal is not a new concept. Take a look at the following letter:

Executive Mansion
Washington
January 26, 1863

Major General Hooker
General:

I have placed you at the head of the Army of the Potomac. Of course, I have done this upon what appear to me to be sufficient reasons. And yet I think it best for you to know that there are some things in regard to which, I am not quite satisfied with you. I believe you to be a brave and skillful soldier, which, of course, I like . . . You have confidence in yourself, which is a valuable, if not an indispensable quality. You are ambitious, which, within reasonable bounds, does good rather than harm. But I think that during Gen. Burnside's command of the Army, you have taken counsel of your ambition, and thwarted him as much as you could, in which you did a great wrong to the country, and to a most meritorious and honorable brother officer . . . I much fear that the spirit which you have aided to infuse into the army, of criticizing their Commander, and withholding confidence from him, will now turn upon you. I shall assist you as far as I can, to put it down . . .

And now, beware of rashness. Beware of rashness, but with energy, and sleepless vigilance, go forward, and give us victories.

Yours very truly,
A. Lincoln

If you were General Hooker, how would you have reacted to this letter? It contains both praise and criticism, which is how most performance evaluations are structured. It takes practice to produce an evaluation that is a constructive balance of the two.

To make a fair assessment, follow the three steps outlined on page 56. It's important to keep on-going records of an employee's performance (i.e. if an employee is expected to complete monthly reports, are they being done well and on time? You might want to make a note each month, so that you'll have a complete picture at the end of the year.)

Out of 500 participants in a management seminar, only 5% said they had ever received a 'good and fair assessment' by their superiors. Many managers tell me that giving performance appraisals is the most difficult aspect of their job. So most people feel that they don't give, or get, a satisfactory evaluation of their job performance.

Practice makes perfect

You can improve your own evaluation skills by using the three-step method in evaluating every day situations. The next time you have to make a purchase, weigh a risk or an opportunity, or assess a person or product's performance, practise describing the object of your evaluation, setting up a list of standards, and comparing the object to the list.

Before going on to the next chapter, make a list of the positive actions you can take today to improve your evaluation skills.

10

SUCCESS FACTOR 7:
Foresight

'Marketing must be consistently future oriented for a
product or service to survive in a rapidly changing world'

E very business believers in its own growth potential. So all employers
are looking for people with foresight, go-getters who can think in
terms of expanding their markets, creating new applications for established products, or variations on services now provided. If you can
demonstrate to a potential employer that you accomplished any of these in
the past, it will be a strong selling point in your favour. Anticipating
future changes is a must, both for individuals and the companies for
which they work.

LOOKING AHEAD

Since the concept of 'tomorrow' was discovered, man has been trying to
look into the future. But foresight doesn't come from a crystal ball or a
deck of cards. It comes from a careful analysis of present conditions,
along with a realistic projection of future trends.

When you see new trends appearing at work, or unexpected problems
or benefits new technologies will bring, think about how they will affect
you tomorrow as well as today. The idea, in this age of constant change, is
not only to keep up with the Joneses, but to stay ahead of them.

Are you looking for a job with a future? Foresight can help you look
ahead with an open mind. It can help you find new applications for old
concepts. In the medical field, for example, foresight is perhaps the most
valuable quality a job seeker can possess. Biotechnology is a growing field

in which research and development lead to exciting medical break-throughs almost daily. Employers in that area are searching for candidates who can see beyond tomorrow.

Not only high-tech industries depend on foresight to survive, however. The garment and fashion industries, for instance, have always relied on foresight to anticipate what the fickle buying public will be wearing next season. Retail sales buyers have to look ahead constantly so they knew how to stock their shelves to profit from sudden buying trends.

Financial institutions try to predict economic trends, nationally and internationally while real estate developers look for areas where growth potential is greatest. Almost every occupation needs people with the ability to look ahead.

I SHOULD HAVE SEEN IT COMING

If you can foresee change, or the possibility of change, you can start preparing for it. Problem solving is not only an exercise in creativity; it's an exercise in foresight. Foresight serves the same function as preventive medicine. When you choose a diet or fitness programme today, you look for the benefits you'll get further down the road.

Foresight is valuable to you on many levels. As you're developing your career marketing plan, foresight will help you keep moving forward in a positive direction. You need foresight to look at your own interests, talents and abilities, and compare them with the opportunities in today's job market.

Have you ever been in a situation where you said to yourself, 'I should have seen it coming?' Often we do see 'it' coming, but we don't pay attention or we let fear and stubborness stand in our way.

Tony and Jeannette were both supervisors at an industrial plant. Jeannette was on the day shift and Tony was on the night shift. For over a year there had been rumours that the plant was closing. Jeannette chose to ignore them. She'd worked at the plant for 12 years, and had an 'it can't happen here' attitude.

Tony's outlook was different. As soon as the rumours started circulating he began making plans. He took a course at the community college to improve his business and communications skills and complete his degree. Tony didn't wait for the plant to close. He made a plan for himself and began a job search immediately.

When the doors at the plant finally closed, Jeannette was out of work – and Tony reported for work the following Monday at an even better job in the next town.

KEEP GOING EVEN IF YOU CAN'T SEE THE FINISHING POST

Is it possible to develop foresight? Isn't it just one of those things that some people have and most don't? Not at all. Foresight, like the other nine most marketable skills, is a matter of attitude. It requires a mind open to all possibilities, a mind able to imagine the unknown. People with foresight can always envisage themselves in more successful circumstances.

You can develop foresight by being enthusiastic about moving ahead, even if you're not quite sure where you're going. Charles Garfield, in his book, *Peak Performers* describes those people who are consistently successful as always being able to see ahead. 'Peak performers want more than merely to win the next game. They see all the way to the championship.' So keep your mind open – and go for the gold.

Before going onto the next chapter make a list of the positive actions you can take today to improve your foresight skills.

11

SUCCESS FACTOR 8:
Independence

'The more we rely on our own sales and marketing abilities,
the more self-assured we become'

A s companies in the 90s re-structure themselves, the ability to work
on your own is becoming more and more important. The atmosphere in the work place is becoming less structured. Work is becoming
much more project-oriented rather than task-oriented; you make a 'contract' with your boss for a particular project and you decide how you want
to go about it.

The standard work day used to consist (and in some cases, still does) of
coming in to the job, being told what to do and how to do it, doing it and
going home. This kind of rigid structure is disappearing fast. You are now
more likely to be given a specific job to do, but you'll have much more lee-
way in how you go about doing it. You will decide (by yourself or with a
group of co-workers) the best way to accomplish a task in order to complete
it within a certain time frame. How you break down your individual day's
work will be up to you.

Independence is a particularly important characteristic for those who
want to work at home as freelancers or consultants. Such people must
enjoy working alone, and be self-disciplined and self-motivated.

THE GHOST OF WORKING PAST

The old work scenario might go something like this: on Monday morning
Kevin Stanley speeds into the car park and pulls into the first available
spot. He runs into the building, knowing that his supervisor is watching

the clock and glancing at Kevin's empty cubicle. Kevin is hanging up his coat just as Mr Price comes through.

'I need this report on delivery schedules done today,' Mr Price tells Kevin, 'so I can send it over to trucking for their approval. They'll send it back up tomorrow for revisions and then we'll zip it over to production where it started. When you finish that, go and see James for your next assignment, he's got an overload.'

'Sure thing, Mr Price,' Kevin mumbles, thinking that James doesn't know what overload is. He works on the report through the morning, goes out to lunch at exactly 12.30, returns to his desk and finishes his section of the report at 3.30. He gets his next project from James and works until exactly 5.00 when he clears off his desk and runs out to his car in order to beat the rush-hour traffic.

The new scenario looks more like this: Kevin pulls into the car park on Monday morning thinking about the report he'll begin working on today. Kevin will be meeting with two other people this morning, one from transport and one from production, and they'll be working jointly on the new delivery schedules. Kevin called the meeting for this morning when he was given the task of coordinating the project, to be completed and delivered to the big boss by Thursday. The meeting continues through lunch (they send out for sandwiches) and finishes at 3.00. Kevin then goes down to the company gym in the basement and works out for a while. He then hops in his car, picks up his son from school and still gets home inside half an hour, having beaten the rush-hour traffic. While driving home he's thinking of how to implement some of the suggestions his two associates had about re-routing some of the lorries. After dinner Kevin works on the report for about an hour on his home computer, and looks forward to sharing his solutions with the others tomorrow.

The new work scenario is beginning to happen all over the country.

THE SPIRIT OF WORKING FUTURE

If you want to become more independent, don't be afraid to ask questions. It's important to know all the relevant facts in order to understand the significance of the task you're doing, and how it relates to the project as a whole.

You may even have to define your entire job for yourself, as traditional job descriptions become harder to compose. Jobs will be structured around key results – the job description will contain certain goals to be met through that position, but again, how you choose to meet these goals will be yours to decide. This is not to say help will not be available. Being independent doesn't mean doing everything alone, it means being able to seek out those individuals who can be of assistance, and being able to enlist and utilise their talents in conjunction with your own.

Computer technicians, for example, are expected to do most of their work on their own. They may work for a large computer service-contract firm that is responsible for the maintenance and repair of systems for many different clients. When a client calls, technicians are sent out alone to determine the problem with the system or hardware. They have to determine what's wrong, fix it, or know when to call for help. Employers in a field like that are hungry for people who can demonstrate their ability to work independently.

Before going on to the next chapter, make a list of the positive actions you can take today to improve your independence skills.

12

SUCCESS FACTOR 9:
Be A Team Player

'Interdependence and trust are the essential relationship
builders'

T eamwork is a cooperative and coordinated effort by a group of
people in the interests of a common goal. It is a necessary requirement for many of today's 'hot' career opportunities.

In the conventional workplace ideas come from above, and are simply
carried out from below. This structure was, until recently, viewed as the
most efficient way to get things done. In the 90s, however, a time of
worldwide technological advances, efficiency is no longer enough. In
order to keep up with and get ahead of the competition, many companies
are looking for innovative ideas and new ways to solve old problems. Most
of these companies have discovered that small work groups, or teams, are
the answer. The hierarchical pyramid is changing to a team-oriented
structure to motivate and energise employees and allow them greater par-
ticipation in the decision-making process.

Employees at all levels are being asked to make this kind of team
commitment. The days when managers are pitted against each other in
fierce battles for power and position are numbered. To succeed in the
business world of tomorrow, you're going to have to team up to do it.

TIPS FOR TEAMING UP

What makes a successful team? A team is more than individuals working
together. Take a football team, for example. Just because you have the
eleven best individual players in the country doesn't mean you'll have
the greatest team. The success of the team also depends on how the eleven

players support and work with each other. A good football team is much more than a collection of individual skills. Team success depends on the way in which all team members play together to produce a united effort.

A team player gives his or her best to the team; at the same time allowing others to contribute. Teams can't succeed with star players who think only of themselves. Becoming a team player means developing your interpersonal skills.

- Do you know the difference between being authoritative and being authoritarian?
- Can you criticise others constructively?
- Can you take criticism without being devastated by it?
- Do you know how to be assertive without being aggressive?

These are all questions you'll need to answer for yourself as you analyse your aptitude as a team player.

Here are eight tips for successful team members:

1. Recognise that your personal contribution and the team contribution are of equal value.
2. Be willing to help others when asked and be willing to ask for help when you need it.
3. Make sure you understand the objectives of the team, and your role in it.
4. Express your ideas, suggestions, disagreements and questions openly with other team members.
5. Be willing to accept comments and proposals from other team members; try to understand their point of view.
6. Realise that every team experiences conflict; work to resolve conflicts quickly and constructively.
7. Participate in team decisions while understanding that the team leader has final authority.
8. Take pride in the success of your team as well as in your own accomplishments.

WOULD YOU PICK YOURSELF?

The best teams in any sport are those that respect and use the talents of all its players. Each team member has his or her own job to do – but each player also knows that winning depends on everyone working together. A star player can't win the game if no one else is playing.

The first step in building your own team skills is to look around and observe other people. Who has real team spirit? If you were forming a team who would you choose? Would you pick yourself to be on the team?

Or are you like Groucho Marx, who said 'I don't want to belong to any club that would have me as a member'?

Assess Your 'Team Quotient'

Remember back in primary school, when one of the categories on your report card was 'works well with others'? It was important then and it's important again today. Like a football manager, an employer is looking for the players with the best skills – and the ones who will support and work with each other.

Here is a short quiz that will give you an idea of your 'team quotient'. There are no right or wrong answers.

1. How do you feel about teams in general?

   A   I like being part of a group.
   B   I usually feel ambivalent about group activities – sometimes I like them, sometimes I don't.
   C   I usually feel like an outsider, not part of the group.

2. Are you comfortable in a team environment?

   A   Most of the time.
   B   I often feel the need to be careful about what I say.
   C   I never feel I can be myself in front of a group.

3. Do you contribute to team efforts?

   A   I make my share of suggestions.
   B   I give opinions when asked.
   C   I express myself only when absolutely necessary.

4. How do you feel about team leaders?

   A   I respect their authority but let them know when I disagree with their decisions.
   B   Leaders intimidate me and I often pretend to know things I should be asking questions about.
   C   I resent their authority, and go out of my way to make problems.

5. How do you feel about team members?

   A   I am usually concerned about their well-being.
   B   I am sometimes concerned about other members of the team.
   C   I seldom go out of my way for anyone else.

6. How do you feel about other people's opinions?

    A   I respect their opinions, even if they differ from mine.
    B   I usually listen to what others have to say.
    C   I'm intolerant of the views of others.

7. How do you feel about criticism?

    A   I welcome it.
    B   It makes me nervous, but I'm willing to listen.
    C   I avoid it as much as possible.

8. How do you view conflicts within the group?

    A   I think they're healthy, and try to use them constructively.
    B   They make me uncomfortable, but I'm able to deal with them.
    C   I'll do anything to avoid 'making waves'.

9. How do you fit into the 'group dynamic'?

    A   I'm an active participant, but I allow others to work the way they want to work.
    B   I like things done certain ways, but will listen to the ideas and opinions of other team members.
    C   I tend to manipulate others to do things my way.

10. How does the team influence you personally?

    A   I am clear about my personal values.
    B   I doubt my personal values when others disagree with me.
    C   I am largely influenced by the views of others.

Give yourself 5 points for every A answer, 2 points for every B, and 1 point for every C answer.

If you scored from 35 to 50, your 'team quotient' is excellent. You have a good attitude towards the team concepts, team leaders and other group members. If you scored between 20 and 35, you need to improve your outlook towards group and group dynamics, and to take a more active role in team efforts. If you scored below 20, you're probably very much of a loner. You may need to change your style somewhat to work within a team-oriented workplace.

Can you find any examples in your past where you worked as part of a team? Consider your experiences at previous jobs, sports teams, in religious organisations, on student councils, in choirs, clubs and scout troops.

Even your family constitutes a team. Here are some questions to ask yourself about your background as a team player.

- What was your role on the team?
- What were some of the things you enjoyed about being on a team?
- How did you deal with people who were not living up to your expectations?
- Were you able to help other people on your team?
- Were you able to accept help from others?

Keep this important Success Factor in mind when you go into any interview. For every two or three individual accomplishments you mention, bring up one in which you were part of a team. Don't always talk in terms of 'I, I, I.' Be sure to use the words, 'we', 'the team', and 'the company'. Employers do want to know you can work on your own, but they also want to be sure you can fit in with the rest of the company 'family'.

Before going on to the next chapter make a list of the positive actions you can take today to improve your team player skills.

13

SUCCESS FACTOR 10:
Value Added Marketing

'The success of value added marketing lies in knowing
what people want and giving them more than they expect'

C ompanies are still made up of human beings, although it may seem
otherwise in this computer age. Many companies are finding that
because of all the high-tech that surrounds them, the human touch is all
the more important to their customers. The employees *are* the company,
so, when recruiting, employers are looking for people who will reflect and
represent their company's image. We've not only moved into the
information age, we've also moved into the age of the customer service
representative.

This new emphasis on customer service is leading employers to employ
people who go beyond what is absolutely necessary to get the job done.
They want people who give more than what's expected – to the company,
to the customer, and to themselves.

We've all seen examples where exceptional service makes a difference.
My neighbourhood is well-known for its abundance of Szechwan Chinese
restaurants. I've tried them all, and they all have similar menus and high
quality cuisine. So why do I prefer one restaurant to all the others?
Because of the service. The waiters and waitresses are friendly, polite,
and rush to welcome me at the door. I wasn't even going to try this place
when it first opened, because it seemed just like all the others. But I was
standing outside it one afternoon, reading the menu, when the hostess
came outside and invited me in to try the lunch special and have a free
glass of wine.

The caring service that I get at this restaurant makes me feel I'm getting
more value for my money.

A SALES ATTITUDE

Companies today are looking for people who:

1. Know what people want
2. Give them more than they expect

You might think that marketing means zooming in on what's unusual and singular about your product, and then 'selling' those features to the buying public. In reality, successful marketing is finding out the needs of the buying public and figuring out how your product can meet those needs and desires.

As we defined it in Chapter 1, marketing encompasses all the activities that get a product or service from the seller to the buyer. But because there's so much competition out there, it's getting more and more difficult to make any product or service stand out from the crowd. That's why understanding the importance of value-added marketing should be your top priority, whether you are part of a large organisation, own your own business, or are in the process of looking for a job.

Every company today, large or small, is on the lookout for employees with strong marketing skills. This doesn't mean that they expect every employee to be a marketing expert but they are looking for people who give that something extra, people who have a 'sales attitude,' and aren't content merely to meet the customers' most basic needs.

Successful salespeople are persuasive, persistent, enthusiastic, initiators, go-getters. They have the ten marketable skills we've been discussing, and know how to use them for the company's benefit as well as their own. Companies must be market oriented to survive. The more conscious of and knowledgeable about the marketing process you are, the more valuable you become to the company.

This is the attitude of the service society of the 90s: your job is to represent your company, solve your customers' problems and fulfil their needs. That is your ultimate job description, whether you're the receptionist or the chairman. And it's this attitude, along with a 'sales personality', that employers want to see.

Understanding the concepts behind selling and marketing is absolutely necessary for every employee today – not just to get a new job, but also to be successful in the one you have.

THE VISIBILITY FACTOR

Being successful in the job you have requires more than just doing your work well. It requires marketing – just as any product or service must be 'out there' to be seen above the competition.

Everyone wants to get ahead, but not everyone is willing to pay the price – which involves making yourself visible. People who do get ahead are constantly asking themselves this question: 'What can I do to make myself stand out?'

You can use this question as a jumping-off place wherever you are at the moment – whether you're in management or in the postroom, still in school, engaged in volunteer work or looking for your first job. Keep the 'value added' concept in mind: you'll not only be giving more, you'll be adding value to yourself.

Take advantage of any opportunities you come across to make yourself more visible. That means getting out in front of other people. If you're asked to head a committee, join a team, or give a presentation, do it. If your organisation needs a spokesperson, volunteer. If you've been given an award, earned a degree, or received an unusual honour, tell the local paper. Let people know. In order to be successful, you've got to be seen.

That doesn't mean you have to pull publicity stunts, or get your name in the tabloids. It does mean that self-promotion and high visibility should be part of your overall plan for success.

YOUR PERSONAL MARKETING VALUES

You can start to work on your personal marketing plan by examining your self-image – how you feel about yourself and how you present yourself to the world. You want to give potential employers the signal that you understand the importance of value added marketing. According to Michael Le Boeuf, author of *How to Win Customers and Keep Them for Life*, the customer's perception of the business or service is what causes him to buy. If the customer perceives he's being given special attention, he'll return to get that attention again; he'll even pay a higher price for it. If a potential employer perceives that you take pride in your work and are willing to go that extra mile, he or she will be much more inclined to consider you for the job, and pay a higher price to get you.

Everything about you is part of your marketing effort: the way you look, the way you speak on the phone, your business cards, the letters you write. As I wrote in my book *Smart Questions For Successful Managers*, 'Your image is an expression of your best self. It's not something you put on like a dress or a suit. Your image should reinforce all of your best qualities. A strong image almost always reflects certain constants: self-confidence, reliability, the unmistakable aura of success.'

Here are some questions to ask yourself to work on improving your image:

- How am I presently perceived?
- How do I feel about those perceptions?
- How would I like to be perceived?

71

- When I speak on the telephone, or write a letter, memo or speech, how do I want others to feel about me?
- If I were a potential employer, how would I describe me?
- What do I have to offer that's unique and special?
- What can I do to enhance my best qualities?

Our culture teaches us not to blow our own horns. You needn't be arrogant to be successful, but a certain degree of self-promotion is necessary. Don't be afraid to be proud of your accomplishments, to say, 'that was my idea,' or to present yourself with energy and enthusiasm. Remember the old rhyme that goes:

> The codfish lays 10,000 eggs, the homely hen lays one
> The codfish never cackles to tell us what she's done
> And so we scorn the codfish
> While the humble hen we prize
> It only goes to show, it pays to advertise!

Make a list of the positive actions you can take today to improve your value added marketing skills.

14

A QUIZ TO RATE YOUR SUCCESS FACTORS

'The more you know about your product, the easier it is to sell'

H ow many of these ten success factors do you already possess? Probably more than you think. Take the following quiz and find out.

While it's easy to be objective about other people, it is difficult to see ourselves objectively. That's where this quiz comes in. It's meant to help you take an honest look at yourself – not to criticise you for having deficiencies, but to help you plan for your future.

Before you go ahead with your lifetime marketing plan, take a good look at where you stand now. To get the greatest benefit from the questions in the quiz, don't ponder them; go with your first, automatic response. Once again, don't answer what you think is right – choose the answer that best describes you the way you are now.

To help you pinpoint areas needing improvement, each answer is notated with the specific Success Factor the question was testing. When you have answered all the questions, add up the points and read the implications of your score.

1. How do you make important decisions?

    A   I make quick decisions based on available data
    B   I avoid them by procrastinating
    C   I take time to look at options and get other people's opinions

2. You are having trouble creating a new design with your computer graphics package. Do you:

A   Go back to study the manual
B   Call technical support
C   Give up and go back to the old design

3. If you were to work at home, which of the following would you have the most trouble with?

A   Dealing with distractions
B   Working too many hours
C   Lack of support – i.e. someone to make copies, etc.

4. How do you plan your day?

A   Just go with the flow
B   Have a 'to do' list and cross out items as they are accomplished
C   Focus on priorities and allow time for the most important items

5. How would your class/clients/family describe your oral communications skills?

A   Shy, but knowledgeable
B   Organised with lots of information
C   Persuasive and interesting

6. How would your class/clients/family describe your writing skills?

A   A 'creative' speller
B   Logical but wordy
C   Gets right to the point

7. How would you describe your listening skills?

A   Attentive
B   Never listen; always interrupt
C   Listen, but only to the facts

8. How would you describe your analytical skills?

A   What analytical skills?
B   Thoughtful and multi-faceted
C   I see only one side and jump to conclusions

9. You have been offered a job but for a lower salary than you wanted. Do you:

A   Accept it and figure you'll work hard and get a raise soon enough

    B   Say, 'I'm disappointed in such a low offer' and wait and see what happens

    C   Explain why you need more money

10. If you have three choices of where to sit at a job interview, would you select:

    A   Across the desk, facing the interviewer

    B   Alongside the desk

    C   On a nearby settee with the interviewer

11. You have moved into a new city and you need a job. Do you:

    A   Call on colleagues you've met at conferences over the years

    B   Look in the newspapers

    C   Call a head hunter

12. You are a supervisor. You have just instituted a new work flow programme for your staff which has increased production by 25%. Do you:

    A   Write up a report and send it to your department head

    B   Accept it as part of your job and make no mention of it

    C   Write up a report showing how this could apply to other departments as well and arrange a meeting with your boss and other department heads

13. What's the first question you ask at a job interview?

    A   What are the benefits?

    B   What's my career path here?

    C   What is this job really like?

14. Do you feel you work:

    A   For security and money

    B   To get recognition and move up in the organisation

    C   To build a professional career that will span a lifetime

15. If your boss criticises your latest report that took three gruelling months to finish, do you:

    A   Defend yourself loudly because you worked so hard on it

    B   'Yes' him or her, but feel lousy about it

   C   After thinking about it, realise that the criticisms are valid and make the changes

16. You planned a vacation with friends and they've decided to go somewhere else at the last minute. Do you:

   A   Go on the trip you've planned without them
   B   Go along with their new plans
   C   Look for other friends to go with

17. At a party, do you:

   A   Meet everyone
   B   Talk to one or two acquaintances who are familiar
   C   Chat with the bartender the entire evening

18. You're usually a 'casual' dresser, but you've been invited to a business lunch at a fancy restaurant with a strict dress code. Do you:

   A   Decide that you don't want to conform and cancel the lunch
   B   Realise that it's a small price to pay and dress as required
   C   Dress according to the rules but hate every minute of it

19. Your voting record shows;

   A   You vote for the candidate of your choice, regardless of party
   B   You follow your party line
   C   You don't vote

20. Your car has broken down and you were to pick up a friend at the airport. You can't get there on time. Do you:

   A   Call the airport and have your friend paged
   B   Leave your car with a tow truck and hitch a list to the airport
   C   Figure your friend will manage, and take care of your car

21. If someone pushes in front of you in a queue, do you:

   A   Speak up
   B   Move in front of the offending party
   C   Complain to your partner

22. You've been made part of an existing team or group project. Do you:

   A   Feel shy about asking the others for help

B   Do your part alone, thinking your best contribution is to do your own work well
C   Find out what the others' areas of expertise are and how you can share information with them

23. You've been asked to create more work space in a crowded area. Do you:

A   Bring in an interior designer
B   Design a few sample floor plans
C   Find someone who's done something similar and copy his design

24. If you were in college, what kind of job would you look for in the summer?

A   Anything you could get
B   Something easy and relaxing
C   Something related to a potential career

25. If your best friend, who is a sharp dresser, criticises your choice of attire, do you:

A   Get defensive and argue the merits of your own personal style
B   Listen, but do what you want anyhow
C   Realise that there's some truth in the comments and decide to change your outfit

RATE YOUR SUCCESS FACTORS

1. Decision-making   A = 4   B = 0   C = 5

The best way to make a decision is to take the time to look at several options and ask experts for advice (C). In the future it's going to be more important to seek expert help, because business functions are becoming so specialised. The answer also shows you're willing to bring other people into the decision-making process. Many times we have to make quick decisions (A). But it's a good idea to think about the possible consequences. You can't really avoid decisions by procrastinating (B) – they only come back to haunt you later.

2. Independence   A = 5   B = 4   C = 1

Calling technical support (B) is not a bad idea when you're in trouble. While in question 1 asking for advice was the best choice, here a better choice is to go back to the manual (A). *Then* if you're really stuck, you can call for help. Going back to the old design (C) may be easier – but you must have had a reason for wanting to change the design in the first place. If you give up every time you hit an obstacle, you won't get very far.

3. Independence   A = 0   B = 3   C = 1

If you're working too many hours, (B) it's probably because you enjoy what you're doing. But you have to be able to set limits for yourself. You don't want to work all the time. If you need support and find it very difficult to work without it (C), you may be better off not working at home – or you may have to be creative in finding ways to get the support you need. There are always going to be distractions working at home (A). If you find this a problem, working at home may not be suited to your personality.

4. Independence   A = 1   B = 3   C = 5

With people working more and more on their own, understanding and focusing on priorities (C) will be essential skills. Having a 'to do' list is good, as long as you remember to check the list (B). Going with the flow (A) is fine for a vacation day, but if there's work to be done, you'll need to have the planning skills and initiative to get things done.

5. Communications skills   A = 0   B = 3   C = 5

If you are being described as a persuasive and interesting story teller (C), you should get a 5+. That's exactly what a good salesperson needs to be. It's also good to be organised and have a lot of information (B), but remember that too much information is going to be boring and turn people off. If you're very shy and nervous (A), people won't listen to you no matter how much you know. Practise your communication skills.

6. Communication skills   A = 0   B = 2   C = 5

You need to be clear and concise and get right to the point (C). Too many people write too much and too long and it becomes difficult to follow. It's important to be logical, but it's hard to see the logic if you are too wordy (B). If you're a creative speller (A) – study on your own, or take a course to help you correct your mistakes.

7. Communications skills   A = 5   B = 1   C = 3

In the 'information age' listening skills will be vital in order to get the information you need. Being attentive (A) will not only provide you with data; it also shows that you care about people's feelings. Listening only to the facts (C) means that you aren't paying attention to feelings or intent. You can learn to listen for clues in those areas as well as for the words. If your friends and colleagues say you don't pay attention and that you interrupt (B), you're going to have problems. Go back and study the difference between active and passive listening.

8. Evaluation skills   A = 0   B = 5   C = 2

Being open minded (B) is going to be of major importance in building evaluation skills. You'll need to see all sides of the story, be objective and rely on your own judgment in order to make the best decisions. Jumping to conclusions (C) is never a good idea, and usually means you're trying to make a decision without having enough information. If you think you have no analytical skills (A), look into your own life and see how you evaluate people and situations within your own daily activities.

9. Sales and marketing skills   A = 0   B = 5   C = 3

Negotiating skills are also a critical element of selling and marketing yourself. You have a lot of power when you've been offered a job – your future employer is delighted that the search is over. The hiring process is tough and time consuming. In negotiating it's important to pause after asking a closing question or making an important pronouncement (B). This kind of negotiating technique will be a big advantage. If your explanation of why you need the money is a sound one you may get it (C); but by talking too much you may just talk yourself out of the job as well. Accepting the salary and hoping you'll get a raise later (A) is risky. You're in a strong position now – this is the time to ask for what you think you're worth.

10. Communication skills   A = 0   B = 3   C = 5

Communication skills include body language and other non-verbal signals, including how and where we place ourselves for a conversation. In an interview, you want to create a friendly atmosphere. People hire people they like and feel comfortable with. The settee is the most informal and the best choice (C). Sitting opposite the desk (A) creates a barrier between you and the boss and puts you in a less advantageous position. Sitting in a chair alongside the desk (B) doesn't create quite as open an atmosphere, but it's still better than having the desk between the two of you.

11. Communications skills   A = 5   B = 2   C = 3

Calling on a colleague you've met at a professional conference (A) is a good example of effective networking, one of the most potent marketing weapons in a job seeker's arsenal. Calling a head hunter or a placement agency (C) is good if you're just the kind of person they're looking for. It's better to take action on your own. There's no harm in looking in the newspapers (B), but everyone else is looking there too. Working on your networking skills will probably get you further than looking in the classifieds.

12. Foresight   A = 3   B = 1   C = 5

You score extra points for seeing the possibilities of your project, not only for yourself but for the company (C). People who can turn foresight into profitable action will have little trouble succeeding in any field. You are on the right track by showing your report to your boss (A). If your boss sees the possibilities too you might get some recognition – but why not be more ambitious? If you just accept it as part of your job (B) you're missing out on a good opportunity to increase your value to your company.

13. Evaluation   A = 1   B = 3   C = 5

When you're looking for a job, you make choices that affect your future. You need the right information to make the best choice. Asking about the career path (B) might provide some insight into your future with the company. But many jobs, especially with smaller companies, may not have clear career paths. Benefits are important (A), but if that's your main concern, you're probably shortchanging yourself. What you're really looking for is an interesting and challenging job – which is why it's so important to ask questions, and to find out what the job is really like (C).

14. Commitment   A = 1   B = 3   C = 5

Working to build your career over the course of a lifetime is the best route to personal and professional happiness (C). If your main reason for working is just to move up in the organisation (B), you may miss out on the deeper satisfaction of contributing meaningfully in a job you really enjoy. With the pace of mergers and takeovers quickening, working for security alone (A) could be frustrating.

15. Adaptability   A = 1   B = 0   C = 5

In your working lifetime, you'll probably be part of many teams and you'll need to be flexible and open to suggestions. If you're able to deal with criticism and not be defensive (C) you'll move ahead faster. Feeling angry is self-destructive (B). Why say 'yes' if you disagree? Defending yourself (A) shows that you believe in your abilities, but you should determine if the criticism has any validity before you defend your work.

16. Independence A = 5 B = 1 C = 4

Going by yourself (A) means you don't depend on other people for your enjoyment. You get full credit for being able to enjoy yourself despite the change in plans. There is nothing wrong with wanting to share your activity with others; looking for others to go with you is another good choice (C). You get one point for wanting to be with your friends (B), but what happened to your plans? Were you thinking independently, or did you give in to peer pressure?

17. Communications A = 5 B = 3 C = 1

A party is a wonderful opportunity to practise your communications skills. If you make a conscious effort to meet and mingle (A), you may make social or business contacts you never dreamed possible. Building a strong support base with only two or three acquaintances (B) can also be helpful, at least to get your networking started. If the bartender looks like Tom Cruise or Kim Basinger you'll get extra points; otherwise this is not a good choice (C). Nothing against bartenders – it's just that staying in one place for the whole party is not the best way to make new friends and contacts.

18. Adaptability A = 1 B = 5 C = 3

Corporate fit will still be an issue for some time to come, and if you're interested in moving ahead you may have to make some small compromises. It's one thing to stick up for your principles, but quite another to be stubborn and closed-minded. If you cancel the lunch (A) you may be cutting off your nose to spite your face. If you dress appropriately but resent it (C), you'll be uncomfortable during the whole lunch and unable to conduct the business at hand. Realising it's a small price to pay (B) shows you're able to judge each situation as it comes up and make appropriate adjustments.

19. Independence A = 5 B = 2 C = 0

You get 2 points for following your party line (B). It does show a certain degree of commitment and loyalty, but it means you're prone to letting others tell you what to do. Voting for the candidate of your choice (A) shows you make careful, thoughtful decisions on your own and don't take the easy way out. You get no points if you don't vote (C).

20. Reliability A = 5 B = 3 C = 0

Accidents happen. The important thing is to make sure you don't leave your friend stranded and waiting at the airport. By having your friend

81

paged (A), you can explain the difficulty and make arrangements to meet elsewhere. Since you're already too late to pick your friend up, hitching a ride at the airport (B) is not a practical solution; then neither one of you will have a ride home. But it does show that you're concerned, and don't want to leave your friend wondering what happened to you. Your friend will probably survive if you don't show up (C), but this is a very selfish and unreliable way to behave.

21. Communication skills   A = 5   B = 4   C = 2

Knowing how to communicate well even when angry is a valuable skill. If someone pushes ahead of you, you've got to let them know – assertively, not aggressively – that you're aware of what they've done and are angry about it (A). Actions often speak louder than words (B) and moving ahead of the offending party can make you feel better about not just standing by and letting people push you around. If you complain to your partner (C), you can let off steam, but it won't get you back ahead in the line.

22. Team player   A = 1   B = 3   C = 5

It's difficult to fit right into an already existing group. But if you're shy about asking for help (A), it will be even harder to get into the swing of things. People like to help others, especially if you're asking about their areas of expertise. You always want to do your part well (B), but when you're working as part of a team everyone must contribute to the group effort in order to make it a success. The best way to become part of the team is to find out how you can help the others and let them know how they can help you (C).

23. Creativity   A = 3   B = 5   C = 3

This is a problem-solving question, and all problem solving requires creative thinking. Designing a few sample floor plans (B) shows you can see problems from many different angles and come up with a solution. Answers (A) and (C) aren't bad choices, but they involve looking to others for solutions. Asking others for help is better than giving up, but only if you've made a strong effort on your own first.

24. Foresight   A = 2   B = 1   C = 5

You work hard at school all year, so during the summer you want something easy and relaxing (B). If the only thing you want out of a job is cash, this may be the right choice for you. But you're missing a chance to develop your professional skills. Choosing a job that's related to a potential career (C) means you're always looking for ways to grow and develop, and that you have an eye to the future. Taking anything you can get may be the only choice you have (A); jobs for college students aren't always easy to find.

25. Adaptability   A = 0   B = 3   C = 5

How you react to criticism shows a lot about your adaptability. When people criticise you, it means they're asking you to change. If you see this as a threat, you'll be defensive (A) and unwilling to make any changes, even ones that would be to your benefit. Listening to suggestions without being defensive gets you three points (B) even if you decide to go with your original choice. If you admire your friend's taste in clothing and listen to the suggestions (C), it means you have an open mind and are willing to change when someone else makes a valid suggestion.

SCORING

95–120 points

Congratulations! You're an ideal job candidate. You possess most of the qualities employers are looking for and will enjoy adapting to a changing world. Now all you need is to develop your marketing plan, and go after the career you want.

70–95 points

You have done very well, and with just a little improvement you should have no trouble achieving your goals. There is always room for improvement, of course, but you're the type who's willing to make that improvement.

45–70 points

You tend to be set in your ways and are less willing to explore new ground. If you want to succeed, you'll have to learn to be more open minded and willing to learn new skills. That you are reading this book, however, means you're willing to give it a try. You'll need a little more practice, but don't be afraid to go for what you want.

Less than 45 points

To be successful in the years to come, you're going to have to put in some time doing the exercises in the Success Factors chapters. You tend to be a more passive person, allowing others to make choices for you. Starting now, you can make the choice to put this knowledge about yourself to good use. Using this book as a guide will help you on your way to future success.

You can see from the quiz that being prepared for success may not always be easy. There are few absolutely right or wrong answers. Nor is there a perfect response for all the intricate situations that crop up in day-to-day working and living. This book will help you develop the answers you'll need to get ahead in this increasingly complex world.

PART THREE

*K*NOW YOUR PRODUCT

15

YOUR CAREER AND CONFIDENCE INVENTORY

'Success comes from building on your strengths, not from correcting your weaknesses'

THE FUNDAMENTAL RULE OF SELLING

During my Marketing Yourself seminars I often ask people to make a quick list of their proudest accomplishments. One woman, Angela, seemed to be having an especially difficult time making her list, so I asked her a few questions.

'What do you do?' I asked.

She said 'I'm a mechanical artist at a small design firm.'

'Do you like what you do?' I asked.

'Most of the time. A lot of times I feel like they don't appreciate me very much though.'

'Tell me,' I said, 'can you think of a time when you did feel appreciated? Anything out of the ordinary?'

Angela thought for a while, and then described a time when the art director became ill in the middle of preparing a major presentation, and she stepped in and finished the project – on time. The client loved it and went on to recommend her company to three other clients.

After several more minutes of probing and questioning, Angela estimated that her company had received over £900,000 in new business because she was able to complete that project successfully. And she had almost forgotten about it!

Now isn't that amazing? How can a person forget about £900,000?

Surprisingly, Angela's response isn't unique. Whenever I ask for a record of past accomplishments, most people come up with a very short list. This isn't due to a lack of accomplishments – it's because people often forget or undervalue their own achievements.

Angela would have a hard time selling herself to a potential employer because she doesn't know her product well enough, even though the product is herself! The most basic rule of sales is that *you must know everything there is to know about your product*. Buyers all want to know the same thing: 'Why should I buy *your* product? What does your product have to offer that another doesn't?' You must know what it is about your product that someone else would need and want – even if they don't know it themselves yet – in order to sell it to them successfully.

TAKING STOCK OF YOURSELF

I'm now going to ask you to do an assignment involving going over all past accomplishments. 'But I know what I've done in the past', you may tell yourself, thinking you'll skip this chapter and go straight to the chapter on interview skills.

But however good your interview skills are you will still fall down if you haven't done enough preparation. It's like taking a history exam without studying, you may have some general knowledge of the subject, but the specifics are going to trip you up. The same concept applies to interviews. You may know what you have achieved in the past, but a prospective employer will want to know what effect it had on your company, your schoolwork, or your personal life. And just as the history professor could tell when you hadn't studied, the interviewer will know when you are not thoroughly prepared.

You have to take stock of yourself by going back and looking at your past with new eyes. It doesn't matter if you have 40 years of work experience or if you have none. Everything you've done in your life – everything you are – counts. Make a list of your life's achievements. Don't worry, you're not expected to include the Nobel Peace Prize. Perhaps you won an award for selling the most homemade biscuits in your Girl Scout troupe. Or perhaps you designed a new brochure for your father's business, or maybe you were a champion swimmer in college . . .

Taking stock of the merchandise is an essential step to beginning any new sales or marketing campaign. This chapter will help you catalogue your personal accomplishments. I call this catalogue your Career and Confidence Inventory, or CCI.

HOW YOUR CCI WILL INCREASE
YOUR SELLING POWER

Your CCI will enable you to find out exactly what you've done in the past, in order to get a better price for your services in the future. *Your Career and Confidence Inventory is an organised list of all your accomplishments.* It will take time to compile, but it's time well spent. This is the key to your marketing plan, and it's something that you'll add to and expand for the rest of your life.

Here is what your CCI can do for you:

- It's an indispensable reference guide for use in all your communications with prospective employers.
- It will help you to get recognition and promotion in your present job.
- It's the basis for your 'sales' letters and telephone calls.
- It will help build your confidence by reminding you what you've done and how good you are.

DISCOVERING WHAT MAKES YOU TICK

Your CCI will tell you a lot about yourself that employers would like to know. And you won't feel put on the spot trying to come up with impressive stories – you'll be prepared. Susan Boren, of Dayton Hudson Corporation, says that when she interviews people, she tries to find out what makes them tick. She '. . . spends time talking with individuals to determine how they've changed in their work and personal lives, and how they've made choices in their lives . . . This is all done during the interviews.'

Imagine that Angela (whom we met in the introduction to Part Three) is being interviewed for a new job and the prospective boss says, 'I'm looking for a real team player. Can you tell me something about yourself that would demonstrate your ability to pitch in and help?'

If Angela hadn't done her homework, she might not have remembered her '£900,000 emergency take-over' story. She wouldn't have anything to offer as proof of her abilities. But because she'd done her homework, the question didn't take her by surprise.

CAREER OBJECTIVES –
THE HIDDEN BENEFIT OF YOUR CCI

There is another hidden benefit to putting in time on your CCI. In order to take full advantage of the marketing concepts in this book, you'll need to have a clear and specific career objective. In other words, you have to know what you want to do. Just as you can't make the general statement 'I'm going to California' (you have to know where in California you want to go), you can't just 'look for a job'. You have to be more specific. Take a career in computers for example. There are lots of opportunities in this field at the moment. But take a look at this partial list of computer careers:

Applications Programmer
Computer Consultant
Computer Scientist
Computer Security Specialist
Database Programmer
Computer Engineer
Hardware Designer
Office Automation Specialist
Sales Representative
Systems Programmer
Technical Writer
Word Processing Operator

And this is just part of the list! There are many more categories and subcategories of computer careers from which to choose. The more specific you are about what you want to do, the easier it will be to target your marketing efforts to people who are looking for your special talents.

Don't be concerned if you don't have a specific job objective right now. Your CCI can help you develop your job objective – by taking a look back through your experiences and accomplishments, you'll be able to see exactly what you're good at.

BEGIN AT THE BEGINNING . . .

Take the time to think about the events in your life. Write them out in story form; they don't have to be in chronological order. You can go as far back as you like, all the way back to that paper round or the lemonade stand in front of your house. If you have no work experience, think about how you've organised your life, how you've managed on a limited budget, and how you made decisions for major purchases or important life choices. Perhaps you're a young mother who organised a play group for the pre-schoolers in your neighbourhood.

If you're still in school, think about how you organise your study time, how you balance sports and academics, how you decided on your school or course of study, and how you improved your study habits.

If you're already working, think about ways in which you have saved your company money, how you reorganised and raised productivity, how you get along with your boss and your colleagues, and how you developed new systems or improved the old ones.

Don't place value judgments on anything. Don't worry about your writing style – this is a personal inventory, not a submittable C.V. Don't be shy. Include the small and the large, and don't be concerned about applicability. At the moment, you are concerned only with getting it all down on paper.

Here are some guidelines to help you get started, in the form of questions you might ask yourself. Use them as springboards, then dive right in and keep going on your own:

What I accomplished in school:

Courses
How were my grades? _____
Did I get any special comments or commendations from teachers, or academic awards? _____
_____
What was my best subject? _____
What made it special? _____
_____

Clubs or Activities
Did I hold any offices? _____
_____
Was I part of any club competitions? _____
_____
Did I have any special responsibilities? _____
_____
Did I receive any awards or commendations? _____
_____

Sports
What position did I play? _____
How did I do in competition? _____
Were there any outstanding games I remember? _____
_____
How, when and where did I practise? _____
_____
Any awards or commendations? _____

Part time work
How, when and where? _____
_____
How did I balance my job with school work? _____
_____
What did I do with the money? _____

Special Interests
What did I do outside school? _____
_____

How, when and where? _____

_____

How did I balance this with school work? _____

_____

Other accomplishments _____

_____

What I accomplished at home:

Planning and Scheduling
How do I run my day? _____

_____

How do I get things done for myself and my family? _____

_____

How do I keep track of schedules, appointments, social events? _____

_____

Part time work
How, when and where? _____
How did I balance my job with school work? _____

_____

What did I do with the money? _____

Volunteer work
How, when and where? _____

_____

How did I balance my job with school work? _____

_____

Budgeting
How do I keep my 'books' or record my spending? _____

_____

How have I been able to save money for myself and my family? _____

_____

How have I been able to make extra money? _____

_____

Prioritising
How do I decide what's most important in my day? Week? Month? _____

_____

Do I set goals for myself? _____

_____

Do I accomplish them? _____

_____

Entertaining
How do I plan social events? _____

How do I organise my extra time, money? _____

Do I do all the work? Do I delegate? _____

Do I plan the menu, shop, cook, hire a caterer? _____

Hobbies and interests
What are my special interests? _____

How do I spend my 'spare' time? Do I read, travel, cook, sew, write, work out, build furniture, sing, etc? _____

Other accomplishments _____

What I accomplished at work:

Organisation
Have I set up systems to help me do my job more efficiently? _____

How do I organise my day's work? _____

How have I helped others be more organised? _____

New ideas
What new ideas have I had for my work or company? _____

Where did the ideas come from? _____

Whom did I tell, and how did I tell them? _____

How were they implemented? _____

Saved company money
What exactly did I do? _____

How much money was involved? _____

Was it an assigned task, or did I come up with the idea myself? _____

Was it a once-only action or a continuing assignment? _____

Teamwork
How do I get along with colleagues? _____

With bosses and supervisors? _____

Have I lead any team projects? _____

Have I been involved in any collaborative efforts? _____

Improvements
What suggestions have I had for my work or company? _____

Where did the idea come from? _____

Whom did I tell, and how did I tell them? _____

How was it implemented? _____

Affiliations, societies, associations
What work-related organisations have I belonged to? _____

Were there requirements to join? _____

Did I participate or hold any special office? _____

Do I contribute to any volunteer activities? _____

Have I written for, or been featured in, the newsletter? _____

SKILLED AND UNSKILLED LABOUR

Many people today consider themselves 'unskilled labour' because they don't have a lot of work experience, or because they don't know how to do anything else. What they don't realise is that they may already possess the most important skills they'll ever need – skills they use every day at home and work. And skills that are becoming more and more appreciated as the nature of work is changing.

Almost everyone's job is being affected by the demand for higher skill levels. It used to be that a petrol station attendant was required to know how to pump petrol, check the oil and give the correct change. Now the same attendant may never even touch the petrol pump or even step out of the glass-enclosed booth. But he or she needs to know how to handle credit cards, how to run a computer, even how to manage the mini-grocery store.

'It amazes me,' one manager recently told me. 'These kids come out of school thinking they're so smart. But ask them to write up a simple report or memo – they don't know how to do it.' I've heard other complaints, from 'No one has any initiative these days,' to 'I don't know what to do with this guy. When it comes to computers, the kid's a genius, but he doesn't know how to relate to people.' These employees were lacking in basic skills.

Skilled workers are traditionally defined as those that have technical expertise in a particular (and narrow) field. But there are other, more basic abilities, that most people do not take into account in the search for their own job qualifications.

These abilities are universal; they apply no matter what job you are doing. They allow you to function responsibly and responsively in any work situation, and are the skills that are becoming more and more valuable as the workplace continues to change.

Why? Because they are transferable skills – they go with you from promotion to promotion, from company to company, even from one career to another.

Your selling points

Although we looked at ten of the most universally marketable skills in Part Two, there are many more skills applicable to any job or career you may pursue.

Here is a list of basic transferable skills and abilities, or 'selling points'. Go back over your CCI then tick each one that applies to you. Can you:

Analyse and edit written material	_____
Carry out research	_____
Conduct surveys	_____
Analyse and evaluate ideas and presentations	_____
Identify problems	_____
Develop new approaches to problems	_____
Help people with their problems	_____

Supervise and lead others _____
Motivate others _____
Evaluate and appraise others at work or in interviews _____
Observe, inspect, review work of others _____
Plan and organise _____
Work on long-term projects (i.e. persevere) _____
Meet work deadlines _____
Think logically _____
Manage time _____
Set goals _____
Work on more than one thing at a time _____
Cope with stress _____
Delegate _____
Teach or instruct others _____
Take risks _____
Willing to learn _____
Sense of humour _____
Make decisions _____
Work in a team _____
Design and instigate _____
Prioritise _____
Use a computer _____
Speak in public _____

Are you:

Patient _____
Assertive _____
Enthusiastic _____
Design oriented _____
Inventive or creative _____
Innovative _____
Resourceful _____
Economical _____
Accurate _____
Attentive to detail _____
Efficient _____
Adaptable _____

A PORTABLE TOOLBOX OF SKILLS

If you have an array of tools before you, and you know how to use them all, you can choose the ones best suited to the task at hand. If you know what a screwdriver is, and know how to use it, you won't waste time picking up a hammer.

The skills you have checked off are your strongest selling points. Suppose an employer doesn't want to employ you because you don't have work experience that directly relates to the job opening. He or she says, 'I'm looking for an experienced administrative assistant. You've never done this before.' How would you answer?

It may be true that you don't have the experience, but if you've done your inventory, you know what skills you have. You know you can organise, prioritise, think logically and accurately; you're resourceful and detail oriented, you have a willingness to learn. These are important skills in any job. You'll sell yourself by demonstrating how you have used these skills and abilities in your past accomplishments.

These are the skills that, separately and together, allow you to work confidently and effectively in any situation. They make you *valuable*; they enhance job satisfaction, increase productivity and give you the competitive edge.

A skill is defined as anything that you can learn to do competently; a developed aptitude or ability. Any of the skills on the check list can be taught, practised and mastered effectively. The more you use them, the easier they become. And you can practise most of them in all your daily activities.

Discovering abilities and skills that can be transferred from one job or career to another is the main reason you're writing your CCI.

Kathryn is a single parent who created beautiful Christmas ornaments at home. She took this skill to a major women's magazine and became a contributing editor in their crafts department. And Dan, who for years had been a popular high school guidance counsellor, used his knack for helping people to begin a career as a training and development executive in a large utility company. Kathryn and Dan discovered their portable skills after writing their CCIs.

Now that you have a good idea of the portable skills you possess, are you ready to go out and sell them? Not quite. You can't just go out and hand an employer a list of every single skill you've ever mastered. Remember the concepts of marketing: you have to know what he or she is looking for and how your product can help solve his or her problems. The next chapter will let you in on one of the sure-fire selling secrets used by all the top sales professionals: benefit selling.

16

BENEFIT SELLING:
The Real Reasons Employers Say Yes

'People want to know the features, but they buy
for the benefits'

'I have some swampland in Florida I want to sell you,' I say.

'Not interested,' you answer, wisely.

'It's more than 50 acres and filled with mosquitoes and alligators,' I say.

'Not interested,' you say.

'It's very cheap,' I say.

'Still not interested,' you say.

'It comes with a map,' I say.

'So what?' you say.

'So,' I say, 'this map shows the way to the Fountain of Youth, which lies in the centre of the swamp.'

'It does?' you say.

'Yes, it does,' I say, 'and not only will this Fountain of Youth keep you young and healthy, it will make you millions of pounds as well.'

'It will?' you say.

'Guaranteed,' I say. 'Plus, you'll be the envy of everyone you know and win the Nobel Peace Prize by allowing only those heads of state who sign a global peace treaty access to your Fountain.'

'I'll buy the swampland,' you say.

Not an easy sale, but I did it. And what made you buy? It wasn't the 50 acres, I'm sure, or the mosquitoes or alligators. It wasn't the map. It wasn't even the Fountain itself. You bought this swampland because it holds the promise of health, wealth, fame and power. You didn't buy because of what the swampland *is*, you bought because of what it could *do for you*.

The 'what's in it for me?' principle

The only reason you'd ever buy that swampland – or anything else, for that matter – is because *there's something in it for you*. The only reason an employer will hire you for a particular job is because *there's something in it for him*. You have to find out what that something is. That's how you make the sale.

The most successful salespeople rely on what is known in the sales trade as 'benefit selling'. They know that all customers are asking themselves one simple question before they buy anything – 'What's in it for me?' And they know they'll have to answer this question before they can make the sale. The secret of successful benefit selling is knowing the difference between features and benefits.

Features are used to describe what a product or service is. *The features of a product remain the same for everyone*. A green and blue plaid shirt that buttons down the front is always a green and blue plaid shirt that buttons down the front, no matter who buys it. If you hate plaid, or if you prefer pullovers, you probably won't buy this shirt. But if the green in this shirt brings out the green in your eyes, and perfectly matches the new outfit you bought last week, the sale is made.

The benefits of a product change for each person who considers the purchase. People want to know the features, but they buy for the benefits. People don't buy air conditioners because they love having a big brown box sticking out their window. They buy air conditioners to be more comfortable during the hot summer months.

My husband loves to fish in his spare time; I enjoy jogging and bicycle riding. A few years ago, a travel agent was trying to convince us to go to a beautiful new resort that had just opened in the Bahamas. He described all of its best features: the rooms, the location, the casinos and the reasonable price. But we'd already been to the Bahamas. We don't gamble, and for the same money we could have gone somewhere we hadn't been before.

'The fishing is really spectacular down there this time of year,' the travel agent said, and my husband was ready to go. I still had my doubts. The travel agent made a phone call. 'The beach is perfect for jogging,' he said, 'and the hotel rents bikes to guests for a very small fee.' We went to that resort and both had a wonderful time, each for our own reasons.

Here's a short list of a table's features and benefits. See if you can tell which is which:

	Feature	Benefit
1. The table has 4 legs	___	___
2. The table is lightweight so it can be moved easily	___	___

	Feature	Benefit
3. The table is white with black trim	———	———
4. The table has a formica top	———	———
5. The table can be cleaned easily with paper towels and glass cleaner	———	———

1, 3 and 4 are features. 2 is a benefit, and 5 is both a feature and a benefit. Get the idea? Try it yourself. Take any familiar object around the house and see if you can describe its features and benefits.

FOCUS ON THE BUYER

People 'buy' for their own reasons. Whether they take you on as a full-time employee, a freelancer or an outside consultant, prospective employers will be 'buying' your services, and they will buy for *their* reasons, not yours.

Imagine that you are an importer of French perfumes, and you're looking for an administrative assistant. You're out of the office frequently; you're slightly disorganised and you need someone who can use the computer.

You see several candidates who all seem responsible, organised, and have good knowledge of the software you use. And they all *want the job*. What would make you hire one above the rest? As it turns out, two of the candidates speak French, a big benefit to you. That narrows the field. In the end, you go with the candidate who can start on Monday, because it's important that you get someone *now*. You didn't hire this person because he wanted the job more than the others. You hired him because he filled more of your needs than the other candidates did.

Any interviews you go on, any letters you send, any phone calls you make, must be focused on what your employer needs and what problems he needs to have solved. The more you can tap into this, the more he'll want to hire you. Your reasons for wanting a new job or career are not important to a prospective employer. You'll be hired only if you fill their requirements and satisfy their needs.

Have you ever seen an advertisement that read:

COME IN AND BUY MY SHOES.
THEY'RE EXPENSIVE,
BUT I NEED TO MAKE A LARGE PROFIT.
IF YOU BUY THESE SHOES,
I'LL MAKE A MILLION DOLLARS.

You would never buy shoes just so that someone else could make a lot of money. You might, however, respond to an ad that read:

> COME IN AND BUY MY SHOES.
> THEY'RE EXPENSIVE,
> BUT THEY'RE THE MOST
> COMFORTABLE SHOES
> YOU'LL EVER WEAR.
> IF YOU BUY THESE SHOES,
> YOU'LL FEEL LIKE A MILLION DOLLARS.

SECRET REASONS WHY EMPLOYERS 'BUY'

Do you know what makes employers 'buy'? They buy (or employ) for their own emotional reasons. This has always been true and will remain true no matter how many technological advances the future holds. So while you may have to reshape your attitudes and learn new skills to remain a marketable 'product', the tricks of the selling trade remain the same.

There are many reasons why people buy (or say yes, or make a commitment), but there are four major categories:

1. Money: people are always concerned with making a profit and/or avoiding losses. Everyone wants to make money or save money; this is why bargains were invented. More importantly, this is why, as I'll explain further in the next chapter, it's vital to link your past accomplishments to bottom line pound results. Can you show that you've been able to save money in the past, either for yourself or someone else? Can you apply that ability to a potential employer's present needs?

2. Recognition and acceptance by others: we always search for ways to improve our relationships with others. Employers need to feel that employing you will enhance their recognition and acceptance, because if you turn out to be a disappointment, it will reflect badly on them. Will the decision to hire you be a popular one? Will you fit in with the rest of the team?

One of my consulting assignments brought me to the office of a mid-level manager in a large financial conglomerate. As we were talking, her supervisor walked by and poked his head in the door.

'Sorry to interrupt, Mary,' he said, 'but I just wanted to say that the new man you hired last month is doing a terrific job. Glad to have him with us. Congratulations – you picked a good one.'

Needless to say, Mary was thrilled. And the next time her performance was evaluated, you can be sure that this hiring decision was rewarded.

3. Feeling good: self-acceptance, physical and mental health are extremely important. People need to feel good about themselves, to take pride in what they do, their reputation and their position. Can you assure an employer that he or she is making a smart decision by employing you? Can you demonstrate that you will relieve some worry or solve some problem?

A colleague of mine, a time management consultant, is a very calm, soft-spoken gentleman, with an aura of authority about him. Many highly stressed executives in the midst of chaos use his services because, they say, 'just having him around lessens the tension'.

4. Looking good: We are, more so in the last decade than ever before, concerned with how we look. We want to buy products that enhance our appearance and the way we feel about ourselves. People want to associate with other people who look good. Employers want to employ people who take pride in themselves and their appearance, and have a style that matches their company's. Do your looks and demeanour reflect the way you think about yourself and the way you'd like others to see you?

Translating Features into Benefits

In order to appeal to a prospective buyer's emotional needs, you need to know how to translate the features of your 'product' into benefits. Never assume that she can figure it out for herself. Always make the connection between what you can do and how it will help the employer. A potential employer doesn't want (or need) to know exactly what you did in your previous job unless she also knows the *results* of what you did. She needs to see your past in relation to her future; to see the results of your accomplishments in terms of how you might be able to produce similar results for her.

Imagine you last worked for a toothbrush manufacturer in the design department. The company brought out a revolutionary new design that wasn't selling because the brushes wouldn't fit in standard toothbrush holders. You designed a plastic adapter that could be manufactured inexpensively and allowed the curved-handled brushes to fit into those little round holes. Suddenly these brushes (which had previously been bought only by a few novelty stores and the boss's mother) were selling like hotcakes in a new package that included your plastic handle-adapter.

Your prospective employer asks you what was your most important contribution to your last job. You say, 'I designed the little plastic adapters that make Acme Curved-Handled Brushes fit into the little round holes.'

True, that's what you did. But the employer will probably say, 'Thank you very much, it's been a pleasure to meet you,' and that will be that.

You make another attempt. 'I'm a very good designer,' you say. 'My designs are aesthetically pleasing as well as practical and economical.'

Better. But the prospective employer is still not impressed.

However, if you were to add, 'My design for the plastic handle adapter enabled the company to repackage the item and *sell three times as many brushes* as they had before,' the prospective employer would undoubtedly consider you strongly for the position.

It's not enough merely to describe what you did on the job – or even to try to convince someone how good you were at it. You must get to their bottom line – why employing you would benefit them.

Now that you're familiar with this important concept of the selling game, it's time to get specific. We're going to go back to your CCI, look for your most marketable skills and Success Factors, and package them into a formidable selling tool.

17

THE AAA'S OF SELLING YOURSELF

'You sell a product best by selectively emphasising features and customising benefits'

Y ou walk into a prospective employer's office. She offers you a seat. After a few minutes of small talk she says, 'Tell me about yourself.'. What are you going to say? Are you going to tell her your whole life story, from the lemonade stand to yesterday's achievements?

Not a good idea. You have to be selective.

If you were selling your life as a book, you'd have to highlight and summarise the important (and relevant) parts to put on the book jacket. This is essentially what you're going to do next: go back through your CCI and pick out the parts that accentuate your strengths. Then you'll compose your 'book jacket' copy, concentrating on features and benefits.

LEARNING YOUR AAAs

Go back to your CCI and look at your first achievement. You are now going to divide it into three distinct sections, creating an AAA:

- The ASSIGNMENT to be dealt with
- The ACTION you took
- The ACCOMPLISHMENTS that resulted.

Let's take a simple example. John was a scholarship student at a top university. He was required to maintain at least a 3.0 grade point average in order to keep his scholarship. During his first year, all of his mid-term exams fell within a two-day period.

John's *Assignment* (the situation behind his actions, or *why* he did what he did) was to take and pass all his exams.

The *Action* John took (or *how* he resolved a conflict or solved a problem) was to design a prioritised study schedule that let him know exactly how much time he had for each course, which subjects required the most study, and what specific topics he needed to cover in each subject.

The *Accomplishment* (or *what* actually happened due to the actions he took) was that John not only passed all his exams, he achieved a 3.5 grade point average for the term.

Writing your AAAs takes practice. But before we go into that, let me share some other sample AAAs with you to give you an idea of how they work:

Example 1. Brian, a production manager at a large cosmetics firm, was faced with escalating prices on the plastic containers his company used. His *Assignment* was to find a way to cut back these costs.

Brad set up a negotiating session with the plastics people. His *Action* was to propose a new long-term purchase agreement with a restructured pricing plan that reduced the price per container. This was a win/win solution, and the plastics supplier readily agreed.

The *Accomplishment*: Brian saved his company more than £250,000 in the next financial year.

Example 2. Donna, a student at a small college was informed that funding for a grant she had been counting on was not available. Donna's *Assignment* was to raise the additional £3,000 she now needed for her tuition.

Donna already had a part-time job working in a small real estate agents. Her *Action* was to negotiate a raise for her work in the office. She also made an agreement that for a nominal fee (to cover electricity costs, etc.) she could use their computer evenings and weekends to make extra money typing papers for students.

The *Accomplishment* was that she earned the £3,000 she needed, plus additional spending money.

Example 3. Gary's *Assignment*, as a supervising social worker, was to solve the problem of the necessary, but too costly and time-consuming, in-person consultations.

His *Action* was to develop written guidelines and to train his staff to use better questioning skills and more effective consulting techniques.

His *Accomplishment* was to reduce the time of each visit by about a third, saving over 3,900 man-hours per year.

Continue on with your own AAAs. Keep listing your accomplishments: think of all the different kinds of problems you have solved, and how you came to the solutions.

Be on the lookout for transferable skills and saleable Success Factors. To help you get started, here are 14 important areas to consider:

1. *Money:* Employers are always looking for people who know how to save, or make, money. Think of a time when you saved money for your company, family or organisation.
   How did you do it? _____

   _____
   When? _____
   Where? _____
   Was there a time when you made money for your company, family or organisation? How? _____

   _____
   When? _____
   Where? _____

2. *Time:* Second only to money, time is of the essence to every prospective boss. Was there an action you took that increased productivity or saved time for your company, family or organisation? _____

   _____
   When? _____
   Where? _____

3. *Efficiency:* Employers want to know they're employing someone who can work speedily, logically and accurately. Can you think of a problem you solved in such a manner? _____

   _____
   How did you go about it? _____

   _____

4. *Organisation:* Employers, especially those who are a bit disorganised themselves, want people who can see a job through from beginning to end and keep track of all the component parts. What event, activity or project have you planned and implemented from beginning to end? ___

   _____
   How did you organise it? _____

   _____
   How did it turn out? _____

   _____

5. *Making Improvements:* Just because something's 'always been done' a certain way, doesn't mean it's the best way to do it. Employers want candidates who can recognise areas for improvement. Have you ever

observed the way something was being done and figured out a better way to do it? _____

What was the old way? _____

How did you improve it? _____

What were the results? _____

6. *Teamwork:* This is one of the most marketable success factors. Employers want to know that you can work well with others. Were you ever involved with any team projects, sports or activities? _____

What was your 'position' or function on the team? _____

How did you and your team work to solve a particular problem? _____

What were the results? _____

7. *Innovation:* A creative spirit is a valuable commodity in a service society. The only way to keep up with competition is to keep coming up with new ideas. Have you ever come up with a new idea for your company, family or organisation? _____

Where did the idea come from? _____

Did it solve a particular problem? _____

What were the results? _____

8. *Hiring or Recruiting:* As we discussed earlier, most people lack essential skills in this area. If you have experience here, it can be a strong selling point in your favour for managerial or supervisory positions. Have you ever hired people or recruited volunteers for your company or organisation? _____

How did you got about it? _____

What were the results? _____

9. *Public Speaking:* Good communications skills are a highly prized and marketable Success Factor. Did you ever have occasion to speak in public? _____
For what reason? _____
How did you prepare yourself? _____
_____
What were the results? _____
_____

10. *Writing Skills:* Written communications skills are also highly valued. Many jobs require you to write reports, send memos, etc. Did you ever use this skill at school, on a previous job, etc? _____
_____
What was the purpose? _____
_____
What were the results? _____
_____

11. *Risk Taking:* This doesn't mean employers are looking for people willing to jump off cliffs at a moment's notice. Sometimes taking a risk can involve accepting a position at a small but growing firm rather than a large, established company. What was the last 'risky' situation you were involved in? _____
_____
Why did you decide to do it? _____
_____
What were the results? _____
_____

12. *Adaptability:* Change is all around us these days, and employers need to know that you can handle various kinds of situations. Think of a time when you were called on to be flexible or adapt to a new situation: _____
_____
How did you handle it? _____
_____
What were the results? _____
_____

13. *Helping Others:* Growing career fields, such as health services and legal and medical assistants, need people who are concerned with others. Think of a time when you helped someone in your company, family or organisation: _____
_____

Why did they need assistance? _____

_____

How did you help them? _____

_____

What were the results? _____

_____

14. *Perseverance:* Prospective employers want to know that if you're handed an assignment, you'll be able to see it through to the end. Think of a time when you completed a particularly difficult task:

_____

What were your challenges or obstacles? _____

_____

How did you handle them? _____

_____

What were the results? _____

THE ASSIGNMENT:
THE IMPOSSIBLE MISSIONS FORCE

In order to make a prospective employer aware of the value of your accomplishments, you've got to let him know what the original problem was and how you rose to the challenge and tackled the assignment.

We take action because there is a specific problem, need or desire. Why does a company suddenly become aware of customer service? It's not because they want all their customers to 'have a nice day'. It's because they're losing business due to inept or inefficient service. Why does a secretary develop a new filing system? It's not because she has no other work to do; it's because she's spending too much time searching for files. So when you write the Assignment, relate it to a specific problem.

An assignment doesn't always come from someone else. Very often the assignment can be self-directed. It arises out of a situation, condition or problem; something you've seen that no one else has seen; something that needs adding, correcting or eliminating. Top corporate executives seek people who see needs no one else has spotted.

THE ACTION:
TAKE THE BALL AND RUN WITH IT

The purpose of the action step is to state concisely what steps you took to fulfill the Assignment. The idea is to tempt your prospective employer to want to know more, to be interested enough to talk to you.

Use dynamic words and strong action verbs. Don't write 'I worked on this programme.' It's much better to say, 'I implemented, or organised this project.' It's better to say 'I analysed' rather than 'I saw', or 'I designed and created' rather than 'I wrote' or 'I did'. 'I trained' is better than 'I showed' or 'explained'. Use a good dictionary and thesaurus and discover the most potent action verbs. Here is a sample list of action-oriented verbs to use in your AAAs:

accelerated	enhanced	persuaded
adapted	enlarged	planned
addressed	established	presented
analysed	exceeded	proposed
arranged	executed	provided
assembled		
attracted	facilitated	recruited
	formulated	reduced
budgeted		refined
	illuminated	renewed
charted	illustrated	reorganised
collected	implemented	reported
compiled	improved	researched
completed	increased	restructured
conceived	initiated	revised
concluded	instructed	
constructed	invented	simplified
contracted	investigated	sold
contributed		solved
controlled	managed	started
coordinated	marketed	strengthened
corrected	maximised	stimulated
created	minimised	summarised
	motivated	supervised
decreased		systematised
demonstrated	negotiated	
designed		
developed	obtained	terminated
devised	operated	took charge
diagramed	optimised	took over
directed	organised	trained
documented	originated	transacted

Focus on your own effort and contributions. Your Action must affect the situation: it should solve the problem.

Do give credit where credit is due, however. If you were part of a team effort, include that information, but let the prospective employer know how you personally affected the accomplishment. Since being a team player is an essential Success Factor, you'll want to have at least one AAA that shows your team spirit.

THE ACCOMPLISHMENT:
IT'S THE BOTTOM LINE THAT COUNTS

Any company that employs you is making an investment in you. It's an investment in time and money and, as any potential investor would, this company will want to know just how good an investment it's making.

Since all companies watch the bottom line, try to show your accomplishments in pounds or percentages. It demonstrates your business sense and your concern for costs and expenses. Did you ever increase your company's profits? Decrease costs? Increase sales or productivity? Put it all down in writing.

Remember that time is also worth money, and good organisational abilities are a valuable commodity. My friend Nicole, a housewife, volunteered to head a telephone campaign for a local politician, a Democrat running in a Republican county. She recruited a small group of friends and neighbours and set up an efficient, organised system covering the entire district. The candidate won – the first Democratic victory in 14 years. The following year, when Nicole was about to re-enter the workforce, she was able to use this Assignment, Action and Accomplishment as an important selling point. Nicole's AAA looked like this:

Assignment: To contact by phone all eligible voters in my candidate's party.

Action: Recruited a staff of dedicated, hard-working volunteers and created a system for covering the entire district.

Accomplishment: My staff and I increased contact with voters by more than 40% over previous campaigns. The candidate won by a 10% margin.

Larry is an ambitious college student who used his organisational and time-saving skills to secure two interesting summer job offers after his first year at college. While a senior in high school, Larry had worked as an assistant in the administrative office. His job was to programme all the students' schedules for the following year. Larry created an easy, efficient system that eliminated duplication and errors and saved the high school many hours of additional work. The principal was extremely pleased with Larry's accomplishments and wrote him a glowing letter of recommendation which resulted in Larry's two job offers. Larry's AAA would look like this:

Assignment: To programme all student schedules for the forthcoming school year, within a limited budget and time frame.

Action: Designed and implemented an efficient, error-free programme for autumn registration.

Accomplishment: Saved the school cost of computer programmer, reduced the number of person-hours needed to work on his project by 50%, and completed the project a week ahead of schedule.

THINKING IN POUNDS AND PERCENTAGES

Think of your Accomplishments in terms of pounds and percentages. It's easy for salespeople or fund raisers to see the direct benefit of their effort, but all employees have an impact, directly or indirectly. Find out how your efforts affect the bottom line. If possible, set up a system of measurement with the financial people in your company. This is important even if you are happily ensconced in a satisfying career: all raises, promotions and salaries are tied to your bottom line value.

Don't wait until tomorrow to start connecting your Assignments to your company's gross profits. In jobs like public relations, advertising, training, and administration, it may be more difficult – but become a detective and find that connection.

Samantha, an advertising copywriter, created a new slogan for an old client and as a result the client signed on for two more years. Samantha discovered that signing this client for two years had improved the company's bottom line by £820,000.

This extra effort, this little bit of research can make all the difference between an average AAA and a great one – one that not only gets you an interview but a job offer.

Make sure you have listed all your Accomplishments in the strongest possible terms. You want to show yourself in the best light. I'm not suggesting you tell anything but the truth. I am only suggesting you pick out and emphasise the most positive aspects of your past experiences. You want to show employers that they would be getting more than their money's worth by employing you.

Your Accomplishment may involve a small number. For example, you may have saved yourself or your company only £100 – but if your spending limit was £200, you saved 50% of your whole budget! Fred has £200 to spend on books in college. He searched carefully through used books and books for trade and spent less than £100. His AAA might go like this:

Assignment: Obtain needed research and background materials on a limited budget.

Action: Instituted targeted search for least expensive materials.

112

Accomplishment: Located and purchased all needed materials, and came in 50% under budget.

Fred effectively used the percentage rather than the dollar amount in this case. As Mae West said 'It's not what you say but how you say it.'

FIVE WAYS TO CREATE PERFECT AAAs

Here are five secrets to writing saleable and marketable AAAs:

1. Have only one Assignment, one Accomplishment and no more than two Action verbs.
2. Use strong, potent, descriptive, tempting action verbs.
3. Your Assignment and Accomplishment must match and complement each other, i.e. the result must solve or resolve the Assignment.
4. Arouse the employer's curiosity by leaving out some of the details.
5. Tie in your Accomplishment to the company's bottom line where you can, using percentages and pound figures whenever possible.

HOW NOT TO WRITE YOUR AAAs

When writing your AAAs you must avoid feeling limited and being judgmental. Get everything down on paper – brainstorm with yourself. No brainstorming session is successful if judgments are made. Judgments curtail the free flow of ideas. You can do your refining and prioritising later.

Another common pitfall is having a great Accomplishment with an unrelated Assignment, so that the problem and the result don't connect at all. For example: your Assignment was to promote three consumer product lines with minimum budget. Your Action was to consolidate staff and restructure advertising schedules. Your Accomplishment states that you increased sales. Although this is a fine Accomplishment, it doesn't relate to the problem of dealing with a small budget. A better way to state the Accomplishment would be to say that you successfully promoted all three lines using only 80% of your usual budget – with a 15% increase in sales.

Many job seekers try to tell their professional life story in one AAA; they become too detailed and too wordy. Here's an example of what not to do:

'Our company was understaffed and morale was very bad. No one had been able to solve the problem during the last year. People were leaving as well. I created and organised a series of employee problem-solving sessions where each employee could be heard. There were 15 employees at each session. I also secured management's commitment that they would send one representative to each meeting and try to solve at least one problem at a time.

This system helped improve morale and no one left and work became more satisfying to the entire staff.'

Try your hand at rewriting this AAA simply, clearly and effectively, using the three headings of Assignment, Action and Accomplishment. Remember to use action words, and to relate the Assignment and the Accomplishment.

Here is my version:

Assignment: For over a year, morale had been an escalating and unsolved problem causing high turnover and absenteeism.

Action: I organised and conducted a series of morale-building sessions between management and employees.

Accomplishment: Within three weeks absenteeism was down by 25%. In six months, there was no turnover and absenteeism was down by over 40%.

Compare this to your solution. Is yours short and concise? Did you include figures and percentages? Did you tell too much? Would it make an employer curious to know more? Keep it short and simple – don't overtell or overwrite.

This ties into the last stumbling block in writing your AAAs: modesty – the reluctance to see yourself in the best light. John Kenneth Galbraith said 'Modesty is a much overrated virtue.' In your job search you have to be your own public relations agent. Advertising mogul Stuart Henderson Britt says 'Doing business without advertising is like winking at a person in the dark. You know what you're doing but nobody else does.'

CUSTOMISING YOUR AAAs

If you were selling a sports car to a racing driver, would you emphasise the car's fuel efficiency? Probably not. Since a racing car driver is much more interested in speed and horse power, you would concentrate on those benefits when selling him the car.

If you're applying for a job as a computer programmer, which requires skills like logic, patience and analytical abilities, you wouldn't stress Success Factors such as teamwork and public speaking.

Whether you're writing your AAAs, sending out letters, or are in an interview situation, it's important to make the distinction between the features of your past experiences and the benefits for your prospective employer. The tendency for many people is to stop at the Action they took, and expect the benefits to be self-explanatory.

Pick the benefits that fit the job. You can restructure your AAAs to emphasise abilities that will be of value to a particular employer.

Let's go back to an AAA we used earlier in the chapter. The first example was Brian and the plastic jars. His company was faced with escalating prices on cosmetics containers. His Assignment was to find a way to cut back these costs. His Actions, or the features of his AAA, were:

1. To set up a negotiating session with the container manufacturer.
2. To propose a long-term agreement with a new pricing structure.

These are the facts, and they remain constant. If Brian were looking for a new job as a production manager for a different company, he would be smart to state his Accomplishment, or benefit, as having saved his company over £250,000. But let's suppose that Brad is looking to change his career, and wants to move into labour relations. He might restructure his AAA by adding that his Assignment was to reduce costs while maintaining good relations with suppliers. His Accomplishment in this case would be that he was able to conduct a win/win negotiation, reducing costs while both his cosmetics company and the container manufacturer got a good deal. For this job, Brad would want to stress his negotiating abilities in his Accomplishment. The features remain the same, the benefits change.

Now, go back through your own AAAs. Make a list of the features of each of your Accomplishments, then translate those features into benefit statements.

BENEFITS WORKSHEET

ASSIGNMENT: _____

_____

_____

ACTION: _____

_____

_____

ACCOMPLISHMENT:
Features (What did you do?): _____

_____

_____

Benefits (How did your actions affect you or your company?): _____
_____
_____
_____

Use this format for each of your AAAs. It's important to know this list backward and forward, inside and out. You want to have as many benefit statements at your disposal as possible. You'll never know exactly what a potential employer is looking for until you are face to face. In the meantime, store up an inventory of benefit statements.

You should always keep a list of ten AAAs in your mind so that you can choose what you need when you need it. Each different Assignment and Action result in an Accomplishment that demonstrates your abilities in certain areas. One AAA may show your organisational abilities, while another may concentrate on creative problem solving.

Think of the confidence with which you can face any interview situation, knowing all the ways you have to solve this potential employer's problems!

PART FOUR

KNOW YOUR MARKET

18
YOUR MARKETING PLAN:
How to Position Yourself for Future Success

'Effective marketing is the result of careful planning'

N ow that you know all about your 'product', you need to familiarise yourself with your buyer.

Who are the people out there who are looking for employees, and how do you get to them? Where do you begin?

You begin with your Marketing Plan. Every business has a plan, a guide for getting customers. Your Marketing Plan will help give your job search direction and a clear focus so that you can proceed straight toward your goals.

WHY YOU NEED A MARKETING PLAN

Once upon a time there lived a brother and sister named Jack and Jill. Jack and Jill went up the hill to fetch a pail of water. After sliding down the hill several times, spilling most of their water and almost breaking their necks in the process, Jack looked at Jill and said, 'There must be a better way.' So they invented non-skid shoes that would stop a tumble mid-fall, and decided to open a retail store called *Kids' Skids*.

'Humpty Dumpty's going to love this!' said Jill.

They found a great spot on a main road. And there they sat – skidless and kidless with no customers except for Humpty and a few of the King's men. Jack and Jill thought of ways to attract customers, but nothing seemed to work. They wanted to send out mail shots, but Nurseryland was a big place and it would be too expensive to target everyone. They placed an ad for non-skid snow boots in *The New Rhyme Times*, but it appeared on the sunniest day of the year, and nobody bought. They didn't know what to do.

One day Little Jack Horner, on his way to a pie eating contest, passed the store and decided to step inside.

'Hey, this store's great!' he said to Jack and Jill. 'How come I never knew it was here?'

'Nobody knows it's here,' Jill said, sadly.

'Why not?' asked Little Jack. 'Don't you have a marketing plan?'

'Well, no we don't,' said Jack. 'Why do we need a marketing plan? We have a great product; everyone in Nurseryland should come to our store and buy our shoes.'

'They would if they knew about it,' Horner said. 'You've got to be more organised about this if you're going to run a business. You have to know what your purpose and objectives are. Of course, you have to know your product upside down and backwards – then you'll know just what kind of people want and need what you have to sell. Last but not least, you have to know the best way to tell people your product exists. If you haven't thought all this out, you'll be stumbling around in the dark like a couple of blind mice. That's why you need a marketing plan.'

Jack and Jill took his advice, and *Kids' Skids* soon became the biggest thing to hit Nurseryland since Mary Mary's *Garden and Grow* seed catalogue.

THE NEWEST SERVICE IN THE SERVICE INDUSTRY

'I'm very happy for Jack and Jill,' you say, 'but first of all, they live in Nurseryland, and second of all, they have a business. What's that got to do with me and the real world?'

To get the job of your choice in the real world, you're going to have to market yourself as if you were a small, growth-oriented business, with an eye to future potential as well as immediate sales. Creating a marketing plan will not only help you get a specific job, it will help you set and achieve long-range career goals.

You are the newest service in the service industry. You are the most important commodity in today's world. Technology doesn't replace the need for human excellence; if you've acquired the essential skills for your chosen field, along with the Success Factors discussed earlier in this book, you'll be in great demand to meet the needs of the country's business environment. But first you've got to let the buying public know you're out there. You need to do the same kind of careful study, research and creative planning any business does.

Just what is a marketing plan? Marketing is a term usually applied to a product or business, and is loosely defined as all the activities involved in getting a product or service from the seller to the buyer. In this case, you are the product as well as the seller. The buyers are the people you want to work for.

Effective marketing is the result of careful planning. A few very unusual products (such as the hula hoop) have been successful by being one-of-a-kind phenomena; another few (such as the board game *Trivial Pursuit*) have become successful because of excellent word of mouth. You too can be successful by accident, but how much more satisfying (and likely) to be successful by design? Creating a marketing plan is the first order of business for any new enterprise.

THE KEY TO BUSINESS SUCCESS

When I started my business as a speaker and consultant, I had no marketing strategy at all. I was leading seminars for the American Management Association, and they would send me out on 'assignments'. Occasionally someone in the audience who was in a position to hire me for their company would do so. Furthering my career was totally dependent on chance; I was always waiting for someone to come up and offer me the next job. It didn't take me long to realise I wouldn't get very far this way. I needed a plan. I worked on my own CCI. I created a brochure to let clients know how I could be of benefit to them; I made a targeted list of potential clients and set long-term goals for myself. Without a plan, I would have moved slowly and haphazardly along. Once I had a plan (which I still use and update constantly), my career moved along at a pace that surpassed anything I had ever imagined!

This may seem a little dramatic, but it's the truth. When you create your marketing plan, several things happen:

- *You create order out of chaos.* Without a clear, well-defined plan, you'll be stumbling around in the dark. A plan helps you keep track of people and appointments and set up a realistic timetable for yourself.
- *You feel better about yourself.* You know you're standing on a solid base, not falling into quicksand. Remember how crucial confidence is to a successful job search.
- *You focus yourself and your thinking.* When your plan begins to take shape you can put opportunities and problems in their proper perspective.
- *You set up goals and measure your progress.* Your plan lets you know exactly what needs to be done and when, and allows you to keep track of what you've already accomplished. A plan helps you set up consistent, thoughtful guidelines to help you achieve your goals.
- *You facilitate the ability to consider alternatives.* A marketing plan allows you to set out alternate routes before hand so that if one tactic doesn't

pay off, another one is readily available and you can continue working towards your goals.

Developing a marketing plan means developing a sense of commitment. If your goals remain vague and ill-defined, you won't know if you're heading in the right direction. Create a plan and follow it, and you've made a real commitment to shaping your future the way you want.

THE FIVE-PART PLAN

Every business, large or small, has a marketing plan. Those flyers you see posted on bus stops and supermarket bulletin boards are as much a part of a marketing plan as is Michael Jackson endorsing Pepsi. Sky-writing your product name over a crowded beach on a hot summer day (especially effective if your product is a cool summer drink), sending out free samples, or sponsoring a charity event – all can be part of such a plan. Your career search marketing plan might include writing a letter to your 'uncle in the business', or handing out your business card at a party.

Just as any business would, you should review your marketing plan every six months or so. Are you on target in striving for the goals you set down? Have you used the tools and strategies you planned to use? Perhaps your goals have changed – in which case you should revise, update or rewrite your plan to fit the new circumstances.

Every business creates its own unique marketing plan, but almost all plans contain the same five major elements:

1. The Statement of Purpose (What It's All About)
2. The Product Description (Who I Am)
3. The Big Picture (My Long Range Career Plans)
4. The Immediate Action Plan (My Short Range Career Plans)
5. The Marketing Tools and Strategies (How I'll Get Where I Need to Go)

THE STATEMENT OF PURPOSE: WHAT IT'S ALL ABOUT

What are my main objectives? What do I want from my work? What would make me happy and fulfilled?

A statement of purpose should contain a brief summary of where you are today, and where you want to be in the future. This section will help you clarify and define goals and set up a reasonable timetable for achieving them.

Barry was a struggling actor and bartender in London. He spent more time struggling than acting, however, and at the age of 32 decided to set new goals for himself. He enjoyed the restaurant atmosphere, but didn't want to remain a bartender. Barry worked on his CCI and came up with a list of 20 AAAs he could apply toward his food-service ambitions. He then began to work on a marketing plan and wrote out his statement of purpose. First, he asked himself what he wanted and needed in his working life. He decided he really enjoyed the interaction with different kinds of people working in a restaurant afforded him. He also felt energised by the constant activity and diverse responsibilities of this type of service industry. His objective was to become a manager of a small to mid-size food service establishment within the next two years. (Barry's completed marketing plan, along with a worksheet for one of your own, appears at the end of this chapter.)

THE PRODUCT DESCRIPTION:
WHO I AM

What are my strongest assets? What exactly am I offering to the 'buying public?' What needs, real and emotional, does my 'product' fill?

In order to market a product, you first have to be able to describe it in such a way that it becomes exciting and irresistible. Describe exactly what it is, and its purpose, so that someone who has never seen it before will know what it does.

If the product is similar to others on the market, the description must include those factors that distinguish this one from all others. Since you are exceptional and unique, and since most potential employers have never met you before, you'll need to provide a general description of who you are and how you can be of benefit to them. You also need to convince them that you are more desirable than the competition.

Your CCI and AAAs are the basis of your product description. All of those accomplishments describe who you are in active and positive terms. Analyse yourself thoroughly and honestly – what are your strengths and your weaknesses? What accomplishments give you marketing power? Everything and anything that would make you attractive to a potential employer should be noted. The more specific and detailed you are, the more you'll be able to identify those qualities that make you 'saleable'. Knowing what your strengths are, and presenting them in the most favourable light, is the only way to convince a prospective employer to choose you over the competition.

Barry's Career and Confidence Inventory gave him the personal insights he used to form his product description. He had done a lot of work over the years in several areas of food service, including being a bartender, a waiter, and a supervisor in a friend's catering business. He was able to use these experiences to build a storehouse of benefit-oriented AAAs.

THE BIG PICTURE:
MY LONG-RANGE CAREER PLANS

What is my main field of interest (law, engineering, manufacturing, accounting, etc.)?

This part of your plan takes into consideration any and all factors that might influence your marketing tactics. What is required here is a study of the 'market' or industry you wish to enter, knowledge of the companies you may wish to join, and familiarity with your competition. This section requires some thought and research – but you can't go forward without it. It's another area everyone's tempted to skip over, but you may miss a lot of opportunities if you do. If you want to make a career out of flying airplanes, for instance, you'll want to know what options are open to you. You decide you want to be an airline pilot. What if that doesn't work out? What if you're not quite tall enough and don't meet the height requirement? Do you have to give up flying altogether? If the only position you know about is 'commercial pilot', you might miss out on many other alternatives, such as flying for the Armed Forces, being a pilot for a freight delivery service, or flying in a corporate jet fleet.

You're limiting yourself by not taking advantage of what others have learned before you. Most people want to skip this step because it takes time and footwork. Make it into a game for yourself. Go to the library, talk to other people, read newspapers and magazines. You don't have to do it all at once.

Become familiar with people currently working in your field and, if possible, those who are also trying to enter it. This is a way to get to know the lay of the land, find out how you might fit in.

Study economic trends. Are you entering a 'hot' field? If so, will it stay hot? In Chapter 20, I've included a list of 30 hot jobs with solid growth potential. Of course, there's no way of knowing if a new technology will suddenly make your job obsolete. The career you pursue should offer you enough transferable skills to be able to retrain easily.

There are fads in the job market just as there are fads in the fashion world, and you should be sure you're going after a growth industry, not one that will disappear in five years.

Study of the overall market is particularly helpful if you want to move up in the same or related fields. If you study your industry, you will find ways of becoming visible within it – and the more visible you are, the wider your network of contacts and the greater your chances for moving up and out. Your marketing plan should include a study of associations, industry trade shows and conferences.

Keeping yourself out front means keeping yourself in front of the competition. Elane, my dental hygienist, has been working in that field for 19 years. Burned out, she was looking to make a career move, but felt limited because she had such a technically specific background. She joined her local dental hygiene association and eventually became its president. One of her responsibilities was to coordinate the regional meeting for the entire state of New York. Using this experience, she is now examining the possibility of changing her career to meeting planning. Because of her visibility in the association, she was also offered a position selling dental equipment at trade shows around the country. She now has two interesting options, all because she stepped out of her office and let the dental world know she was around.

Other considerations in your overall marketing view are the personal factors. Do you want to travel in your job? Are you getting married or divorced, or moving from one part of the country to another? Anything at all that will influence your strategy belongs in this section.

At this point, Barry began a serious study of the restaurant and food service industry. His research told him that this was an area with good growth potential, a 'hot' field that would be around for a long time. He subscribed to trade papers and joined a restaurant association for the London area. Since he knew a lot of people in the business, Barry was able to speak to other managers and restaurant owners. He considered buying a fast-food franchise, or opening his own catering service. Barry also spoke to the Chambers of Commerce in nearby cities to find out what the competition was like in other areas of the country.

THE IMMEDIATE ACTION PLAN: MY SHORT-RANGE CAREER GOALS

Just who is it you want to be working with and for? Who would your ideal 'buyer' be? What kind of job would you be willing to settle for if necessary?

Now narrow and refine your list of job opportunities until it includes only and exactly those that fit your criteria. If you desire a lot of structure and privacy in the workplace, for example, then you would pursue only those companies that provide this type of atmosphere. If you like a relaxed, friendly environment with a greater emphasis on teamwork, your research should be leading towards a looser, less hierarchal company structure.

This is where your plan starts to get specific. You can no longer say, 'I'm looking for a job.' Companies should now have individuals' names attached to them – your objective being to reach not only that firm, but the particular person in that firm who has the power to employ you. Start off with a list of 10–20 people (the length of your list will depend on the industry and the area you're covering). You'll need the name of the company, the name of the specific person with the power to employ you, her correct title, address and telephone number.

Find out as much as you possibly can about each company. Companies have personalities just like people do. Your personality must be compatible with theirs, otherwise the relationship will never work.

Carol is a vivacious, outgoing person with a high energy level. She's one of those people who loves to be with people. When she was interviewed for a telemarketing job in a two-person office, it seemed like a good opportunity. But Carol didn't think it through carefully. She didn't take her personality into consideration. She thought that talking to people on the phone would be enough interaction, but what she really needed was personal contact. Carol soon realised that she needed a larger office setting, and a job that put her in personal contact with customers.

Some companies are extremely conservative and traditional; others are more aggressive and experimental. If you enjoy a more aggressive, innovative atmosphere, you probably won't be happy in a staid, conservative corporation. Do some homework: send off for and study companies' latest reports and accounts to get a general idea of the corporate style; go to the library and look for sources that will tell you how well the company is doing, and who its top personnel are (see page 233 for a list of possible sources). Also contact the Chambers of Commerce in other cities or towns where you would like to work. They will often be able to supply you with a list of local industries.

Barry decided he would look for work in London, Bristol, Oxford and Cardiff. He visited many restaurants and spoke to a large number of people in all the cities he had on his list. (It's not always possible to personally check out potential job sources in other cities – but if it is, it's a good way to get first-hand knowledge of the opportunities and atmosphere a company has to offer.) Barry made up a list of 18 promising restaurants. His criteria included: establishments that had been in business five years or more, a semi-formal or formal atmosphere, good locations, quality service and excellent food. He had names, addresses and phone numbers of owners and/or managers and was ready to move into the action phase of his marketing plan.

THE MARKETING TOOLS AND STRATEGIES: HOW I'LL GET WHERE I NEED TO GO

Exactly how am I going to go about achieving my goals? Where do I begin my search? How do I let people know I'm out there?

When you have developed your product description, your big picture and your immediate action plan, you can begin to select your marketing tools and develop your creative strategies. If you were developing a marketing plan for a small business – selling children's shoes for example – your marketing tools might include radio and television advertising, newspapers, magazines, direct mail, etc. Your strategy would define which of those media you choose, how often you advertise, what percentage of your budget you spend on advertising. It would be based on all the knowledge you've accumulated about the market. In order to sell children's shoes, you might choose prime time television and the Sunday newspaper family section. If you were selling jeans for teenagers, you might want to advertise on Saturday morning TV, or in teenage magazines. You must determine the best ways to reach your buying public.

The same goes for marketing yourself. You choose the marketing tools that are best suited to your 'product'. Do your homework – search out all the marketing tools available to you, analyse their potential for generating leads, and plan your marketing effort accordingly. Your purpose is not just to get a lot of leads; you want to get qualified leads that will move you forward to getting an interview.

Notice I said move you toward an interview, not to getting a job. Though employment is the ultimate goal, your marketing effort is designed to give you as many options as possible. The more interviews you go on, the more job offers are potentially yours.

Your strategy should also include a timetable. Plan out how much time during each day, week, or month you will devote to your search. Is your goal to go out on two interviews a day, or two a week? (This will depend on whether or not you are presently employed.) Make an action plan for yourself, such as:

Sunday: read the situations vacant ads
Monday: answer the ads and set up appointments, go to library
Tuesday: write letters and/or go on appointments
Wednesday: network via the telephone and/or appointments
Thursday: go to employment agencies
Friday: continue research at the library

Your action plan will change from week to week as you progress in your search. Set up rules and deadlines for yourself. Remember, there are no losers in this game, only quitters.

Barry was still working when he decided to change careers, so he had to devise ways to structure his time. Most of his free time was in the morning, as his bartending duties didn't begin until mid-afternoon. He decided that his two most effective marketing tools would be direct mail letters and personal contacts. He would also check the situations vacant ads daily in local and national newspapers.

Review your strategy periodically and keep a record of your progress. Which marketing tools have yielded the most leads? Did any have better results than you expected? Worse? Revise your strategy accordingly.

Networking and personal contacts

Statistics show that up to 80% of all new jobs are found through networking. James Clemence, Director of Management Development at Peat Marwick, says that in the future, 'getting a job will depend on your networking skills. It's going to be more and more difficult for job seekers to come face to face with the people who can actually employ them. You must become visible within your profession – therefore networking should be a major area of your job searching strategy.'

The important thing to remember here is that *all leads are worth pursuing*. Not every lead will turn out to be productive, but you'll never know unless you take the time to find out.

Everyone has contacts. I don't mean that everybody knows somebody who will offer you a job. But somewhere along the line, a lead will bring you to someone who knows of a job opening. The most farfetched situations often turn out to be the most interesting.

There's no way to predict who among your contacts will produce the best leads; therefore you should contact everyone. This includes family, friends, old business acquaintances, college professors, your doctor, your dentist, your solicitor, your hairdresser, members of clubs you belong to . . . everyone you know.

Make sure you tell people specifically what you're looking for. Let them know you appreciate any help they can give you. The next person they speak to may just tell them about a job opening and you want your contact to think of you immediately. And if someone says, 'Call me back in a week,' do it. It may not be the brush-off it seems to be.

Make a list of the different reasons you might have for networking, and the people you know who might fit those needs.

Your networking notebook might look something like this (always leave room for additional names to add in the future as your support system should constantly be increasing):

Information Sources
The more I know, the more power I have. Who knows the most about my field? _____

Who do I know who can put me in touch with that person? _____

Who has information I can use to build my skills at home or at work? _____

Who can provide guidance in solving problems, or help me figure out what my next action should be? _____

If I don't know that person, do I know someone who does? _____

Additional Names: _____

Support Groups
Who are the people around me who are 'in the same boat'? _____

Have I done any favours for friends? Who are they? _____

Which of my friends do I enjoy exchanging ideas and experiences with? _____

Which of my friends and colleagues recognise and appreciate my skills and accomplishments? (These are people you can use as sounding boards. For instance why not 'try out' that new idea before presenting it to top management? No need to give away all the details. Present it as a concept to a few people in your network and check the response.) _____

Additional Names: _____

Family, Friends, Acquaintances
Who do I know (don't forget distant relatives) who work in the same or related field as I do? _____

Who, of all the people I know, is the best networker? _____

(Get these people to help you network – they'll love it!) Have I let everyone know I'm looking for a job? Did I tell my:
Friends __   Family __   Doctor __   Solicitor __   Dentist __
Accountant __ Neighbours __ Former Employers __   Colleagues __
Club Members __   Sports Team Members __

Future Possibilities

Who are the people I'd most like to meet (someone I heard speak at a conference, someone a friend or colleague spoke highly of, etc.)?_____

How can I get in touch with those people?_____

Are there any clubs, organisations or associations I can join that will put me in contact with the kinds of people I want to meet?_____

Do I know anyone, or is there anyone I want to know, who can make me think, who will challenge me to grow?_____

How can I find these people? (Networking is very much like solving a puzzle – finding one clue leads you on to the next and the next. One contact refers you to another, who refers you to another until you find that one contact who will provide you with the solution you need.)_____

How can I do my own 'public relations'? Is there a newsletter I can tell about my promotion, successful presentation, etc?_____
A local newspaper?_____
Trade magazine or journal?_____
Additional Names: _____
_____
_____

The information interview

The information interview is one of the strongest marketing tools available to you. Information gives you power. If you're moving from one field to another – i.e. from dental hygiene to meeting planning – your disadvantage is that you probably don't know many details of the meeting planning industry. If you go on information interviews, where your object is not necessarily to get a job offer, you can concentrate on filling in the gaps in your knowledge.

People who would say no to a job interview will often be flattered and say yes when asked for their advice or opinion. However, be prepared in case it should turn into a job interview. I remember going on one information interview with a Mr Stein. A friend had referred me to Stein, knowing there were no jobs available in his firm, but also knowing he knew a lot about the advertising field. While I was sitting in his office, a colleague of Mr Stein's happened to stop by. It turned out he was in need of an advertising sales rep, and he gave me a job interview on the spot. An opportunity would have been lost if I hadn't been prepared for the unexpected.

In an information interview, you'll want to ask questions like:

- What do you like about this industry?
- What don't you like?
- What do people look for when recruiting in this field?
- What associations best represent this industry?
- Are there trade newspapers and magazines I should know about?
- How did you get into the industry?
- Is there a 'normal' career path for people in this field?
- What qualifications are essential to succeed in this industry?

The more you know about any industry, the easier it will be for you to qualify future leads. You'll know what people are looking for, and what qualifications you already possess. You can then tailor your approach in a job interview so that you stress those particular qualifications. You can even quote your information sources as authorities in the industry: 'Stan Philips at XYZ Corporation says you need patience and logic to succeed in this industry. These are two of my strongest qualities.'

Information interviews also serve as practice for job interviews. You can practise your interpersonal and communications skills so that when you actually have a job offer at stake, you'll be prepared and confident in your interviewing abilities.

The situations vacant columns

The first marketing tool that comes to everyone's mind is the situations vacant columns in national and local newspapers. The advantage of these is that you can scan them quickly, covering a lot of territory in a little time. The disadvantage is that everyone else is doing the same thing and, especially in larger cities, the competition can be tremendous. Don't let that stop you. If the job sounds right up your street, go for it.

Get a hold of back issues of the papers if you can. Not all jobs get filled on the first go-around. Many times employers are waiting for just the right person to come along – and it could be you. Look through the entire classified section. Job titles can be deceptive, and a company (or the newspaper) may have placed the job you want under an unlikely heading. So don't limit yourself by looking only under the job title you think you want. For instance, some papers have ads under the 'A' section entitled 'Accountancy – Tax'; as well as ads under 'T' for 'Tax Accountants'. If you want to get started in Public Relations, you might look under that heading – but you might also get a foot in the door by starting as receptionist or administrative assistant in a P.R. firm, and those jobs may be listed under different headings.

Read the business pages of your local paper and research any people or companies that seem interesting. Make a contact – call or write.

Business publications and trade journals usually have very good situations vacant sections, and they are geared to specific industries. These are usually ads for 'insiders' – people who are already in the industry and are looking to change jobs.

Keep the odds in mind when looking through situations vacant columns. There will probably be a large number of people with similar qualifications applying for each position. That doesn't mean you shouldn't apply, just don't be surprised if you get a rejection or no response at all.

Job fairs

Job fairs are a good source of leads. Usually held at a local hotel or convention centre, they give you a chance to talk to an actual human being. These fairs are often geared to entry level jobs, so they aren't for everyone. They can be a good source for information interviews, however, and they give you a feel for the kinds of people you're likely to encounter in a particular industry.

Employment agencies, headhunters and personnel

Employment agencies can be a very good source of job opportunities. The problem is that there are so many around, choosing a good one can be difficult. Don't be afraid to ask questions. Go to an established agency with a good reputation.

Headhunters usually work on executive level positions, and can also be a good source. The problem with both employment agencies and headhunters is that you're not dealing directly with the people doing the recruiting.

Headhunters may be armed with your C.V. but if they just send it over to personnel, you're twice removed from the potential employer! You're the only one who can really sell yourself to the employer, and the best way to do that is to contact him or her directly. (We'll discuss this in detail in Part Five, Closing the Sale.)

Most employment agencies and headhunters collect their fees from the company, so the service to you is free. But make sure you understand any payment obligations before you sign anything, and certainly before you hand over any money. Be wary of any agency that requires money up front, before they have connected you with a job.

Direct mail

Direct mail is the newest growth area in the advertising and marketing fields. All those letters you get at home urging you to buy new products, subscribe to a magazine or donate to a charity are direct mail campaigns.

Direct mail is also one of the best and fastest growing methods available for your career campaign. It is so important that Chapter 23 is entirely devoted to your direct mail effort.

SAMPLE MARKETING PLAN

A marketing plan is a tool to clarify and focus your job search and long-term career strategy. The document is for your eyes only, so don't be concerned with style or format. Make it a plan that works for you.

Here is a sample of Barry Moore's marketing plan:

1. Statement of purpose

I, Barry Moore, am currently bartending full time at Sullivan's Steak House in London. I want to stay in the restaurant business or food service industry in a small to mid-size establishment. My goal is to be in a managerial position within two years.

2. Product description

(This section consists of Barry's list of 10 AAAs. Here is one example):

My Assignment, as a supervisor for 'Fine Feasts To Go' Catering Service, was to revise scheduling procedures to avoid no-shows among the temporary catering staff. These no-shows were often the cause of inefficient service.

My Action was to implement a networking system among employees, making each person responsible for finding his own replacement.

My Accomplishment decreased no-shows by 65%, thereby improving service and efficiency and generating 30% more repeat business.

3. The big picture

1. I will remain in the food service industry.
2. I will subscribe to trade papers and join relevant associations.
3. I will write to the Chambers of Commerce in Bristol, Oxford and Cardiff.
4. I will also look at franchising possibilities in these other cities. Since I have contacts in the catering business, this is another area of exploration.

4. Immediate action plan

My first order of business is to go to the library to find addresses for the Chambers of Commerce and look up the restaurant trade papers, and then to make a list of personal contacts.

I have chosen 18 restaurants to contact for assistant manager positions. There are eight in London, five in Bristol, three in Oxford and two in Cardiff. They've all been in business five years or more, have excellent locations, have a somewhat conservative atmosphere and a reputation for excellent cuisine. I also have the names of three catering services in London and Bristol. (Here Barry would list names, addresses and phone numbers.)

5. Marketing tools and strategies

My main marketing tools will be:

1. Networking
2. Direct mail
3. Situations vacant columns in trade papers
4. Situations vacant columns in newspapers

I'll do most of my marketing in the mornings. I'll have to make some calls from my present job, however, in order to reach people who come in later in the day or work in the evening.

I'll take a week off from my job and go to interviews in other cities I've targeted (all appointments arranged before hand via phone).

I'll set up a special area at home where I keep all my notes and research, and create an organised follow-up system to keep track of all appointments, phone calls and interviews.

I'll set up a day to day action plan, a week at a time, so that I know exactly what to do each day to reach my goal.

YOUR MARKETING PLAN WORKSHEET

Use the following worksheet as a guide to preparing your Marketing Plan.

Statement of Purpose: _____
_____
_____
_____

Product Description: (AAAs – list at least 10)
Assignment: _____
_____

Action: _____

Accomplishment (include benefit statements): _____

_____

_____

_____

_____

The Big Picture: _____

_____

_____

_____

_____

Immediate Action Plan: _____

_____

_____

_____

_____

Marketing Tools: _____

_____

_____

_____

_____

Marketing Strategies: _____

_____

_____

_____

_____

The next three chapters will help you develop your marketing plan. Before you can make any final decisions in planning your job search process, you need to study the market. The following chapters will give you an idea of current economic trends, some of the hot, growth-oriented jobs that are in demand right now, and how to get them.

19

YOU'VE GOT TO KNOW THE TERRITORY:

Trends in the New Economy

'A successful marketing plan is based on
understanding current economic trends'

Congratulations! You've just been hired by Kids' Skids to handle their new line of Jack B. Nimble athletic footwear to the entire Northwest Territory.

You feel pretty good about yourself, and you know a lot about the Jack B. Nimble line, but you don't know anything about the Northwest Territory. The first thing you do is:

A. Get out there and start knocking on doors.
B. Get a map.
C. Call the Chamber of Commerce for a list of businesses that currently stock Jack B. Nimbles, study who they are, where they're located and how they're doing.
D. Go through old company files and look for concentrated areas of past Jack B. Nimble purchasers, study who they were and why they no longer stock Nimbles.

B, C and D are all logical and practical answers. If your answer was A, which is what we all tend to do in the rush of enthusiasm, you'll be spending a lot of time accomplishing nothing. You have to know the territory.

Every sales effort requires background information that includes past, present and future market trends for the product or service you're selling.

Your job search sales and marketing effort is no exception. Before you just go out there and start looking for a job, you should be able to answer these questions:

• Who's employing whom?

- What are the available jobs in your field of interest?
- Where are these jobs located?
- What kind of background, education and/or training do you need to get these jobs?

Knowing your market means cultivating an awareness of what's happening in the economy as a whole – what the trends and social factors are that are shaping our society today and tomorrow, and how those trends affect you and your job search.

THE AGE OF THE SERVICE SOCIETY

No one can know what the future holds in store, but we do know that a new century is just around the corner, and that it will be a century of choice and change. You can expect to hold several different jobs – even several different careers – during your working lifetime. Technology is already giving you many new and unexpected choices about how, when and where you choose to work.

Modern technologies have brought us from the industrial age to the information age: the age of the service society.

What is a service industry anyway? A service industry doesn't produce goods the way manufacturing or agriculture does. You don't end up with a solid object you can ride in, taste or sleep on. Services create economic value without creating a tangible product.

Service industries can range from low-wage minimal skill jobs, such as fast food servers and supermarket cashiers, to high wage and highly skilled jobs in the areas of biological engineering and computer technology.

Twenty years ago one in two British workers had jobs in service industries. Today it is more than two out of three. The main areas for growth are in business and financial services, hotels and catering, distribution, and a wide range of other services including leisure and recreation.

TECHNOLOGICAL PROGRESS

Technology has influenced changes in every conceivable industry and occupation – from agriculture to zoology, from fine arts to meat packing, from plumbing to worm farming. Technology is forcing us to retrain and restructure our ways of working and the tasks we perform on the job.

It will be impossible to advance along with technological progress unless you advance your attitudes towards learning, training and .

retraining. Getting and holding a job will depend on your ability to keep up and be adaptable. You'll have to be ready and willing to learn new skills at any point in your career, and companies will need to be prepared to increase training facilities. Technology may eliminate your job. If you're prepared for change, you'll study a different and newer technology and be able to transfer your skills easily.

If you refused to give up your horse and buggy when the car was invented, you never got to travel very far. But if you were farsighted, the first time you saw an automobile, you opened up a petrol station. Keeping up with the state-of-the-art technology will be crucial to ensure that you and your talents are constantly marketable.

THE CHANGING WORKFORCE

The baby-boom generation (born between 1946 and 1964) accounted for much of the rapid growth rates in the labour force up until the 1970s. Now, the 'birth dearth' generation (born between 1965 and 1978) is causing the workforce to increase at a slower rate than at any time since the 1930s.

This could be good news for job seekers. Employers will have to offer better salaries to attract the best people.

Britain Grows Up

The work force is also maturing. The baby boom generation is growing up while the number of young people is declining. The numbers aged 16–19 in the population will have fallen by over 1 million between 1987 and 1993. In the labour market this means that the number aged under 25 is projected to fall by 1.2 million between 1987 and 1995.

The impact of an older workforce has both positive and negative influences on our economy and employment market. Some of the negative results will be:

- industries that traditionally depend on young people for growth and survival (higher education, housing construction and home furnishings, etc.) may suffer.
- the decline in the number of younger workers may make it harder to start up new companies or for established companies to grow or change rapidly. Older workers are usually less willing to relocate or retrain in response to changing conditions.
- many companies are looking for ways to scale down and reduce middle management. Competition for jobs at this job level and age range will be great.

But there are positive effects as well:

- an aging workforce represents experience, reliability, stability and health, which translates into improved productivity.
- the national savings rate will rise as the population gets older, which is good for the overall economy. Younger consumers are more likely to spend and borrow, while people over 40 tend to save and invest.
- companies that used to employ young people for little pay may have to raise wages and offer better incentives to entry level workers.

The impact of an 'older' workforce is good for both older and younger job seekers. Many companies are starved of qualified entry level employees. If you are just starting out, and show (from your AAAs) that you have the success factors employers are looking for, you'll be a very valuable commodity. And if you are in the older age bracket, and are looking to re-enter the workforce, you can use your experience and reliability to sell yourself to employers who are in need of people with exactly those qualities.

Leonard Kolberg, a 69-year-old retired insurance claims adjuster is now in great demand as a part-time private investigator for several small law firms. The firm gets someone with the perfect background and professional experience they need (to photograph accident sites, interview witnesses, serve summons, etc.). And Leonard remains an active member of today's workforce on a schedule that's convenient to his age and lifestyle.

Leonard used his knowledge of his own particular talents and abilities, along with his knowledge of changes in today's workplaces, and marketed himself to employers who needed those skills and expertise.

But it's impossible to sell yourself in today's changing job market without knowing the trends and influences shaping our nation's economy, and determining when and where we're working and who for.

Commuters v. Computers

Do you fit into this changing world of work we're talking about? Or will you, like the dinosaur, disappear from view to appear in history books as an extinct species that couldn't adapt to a changing world?

Fortunately for humans, we're an adaptable species. If we're willing to learn, we can come out ahead every time. The more you know about how work is shaping up these days, the more choices you have about how, when and where you want to work. Not everyone is looking for a 9–5 job in a traditional office setting. If the job of your choice involves an alternative lifestyle or flexible schedule, use your market research to learn how other people have made these non-traditional choices work for them.

Many people are now choosing to work at home in offices set up in spare rooms, basements or garages. Advances in technology have made it possible to compute instead of commute – to work from home and tap into a company's resources across town or across the world via a remote computer terminal.

Having this option proved to be a perfect solution for one young couple I met, Ellen and Larry Schneider. Ellen is a Regional Section Manager at The Equitable, a large insurance company. Larry is a computer programmer for an accounting firm. When Ellen and Larry decided to start a family, they wanted to find a way to raise a child while they both continued to work.

'Larry's company was just beginning to revamp its human resources programme,' Ellen told me. 'They were making a conscious effort to improve their benefits, including child-care. We proposed a work-at-home plan for Larry. We 'sold' them on the advantages for the company of keeping a valued employee, and they accepted the idea. I'm going back to my office after the baby is born, and Larry's going to be working from home.

'Since Larry now has 24-hour access to his home computer, he can do full-time work on his own schedule. He's doing the same work he did at the office – it's just in a different setting.'

There are drawbacks to this arrangement. Larry may not be promoted as quickly as someone else who is more visible at the office. And spur of the moment meetings with co-workers are no longer possible, so Larry will need to coordinate schedules and go into the office once a week for meetings. But both Ellen and Larry feel their 'sales strategy' enabled them to find a way that works well for both the company and for their family.

'I couldn't really work at home,' says Ellen. 'My job isn't suited for it. And besides, I enjoy the daily interaction with other people. Larry is fine without it.'

You may not choose to work at home either. Human beings are social creatures. We like being with people; we learn from them, we laugh with them. We enjoy seeing new faces now and again. But the operative word here is *choice*. Advances in technology have given us the freedom of choice – and the choices we make will in turn help determine the future technological advances.

The temporary life

One of the choices that many people are now making is to join the growing numbers of temporary workers. There has been constant and phenomenal growth in the temporary industry in the past few years, and the future promises more of the same.

Many temporary workers are offered permanent positions once they have proven themselves on the job. Using your sales skills, you can negotiate for more and get it. The more you can sell yourself and your success factors to companies, the more they'll value your worth.

Being a temporary worker has its down side – you don't usually get any company benefits such as insurance, sick leave or holiday pay. But even that is changing, as many temporary agencies are offering benefits of their own. The advantage of this kind of work is that it gives you near total freedom about when and where you work. If you have school-age children, for example, you can work when they're in school and stay at home when they're on holiday. That is just how Jane, a mother of two, manages to bring in extra income and still have time off when her children are at home.

Part-timers

The part-time workforce is becoming a major factor in this country. There are already over 5 million part-time workers, a quarter of all employees, and this number is likely to increase in the years ahead. Companies will continue to institute broader part-time and flexible schedule plans enabling them to match the size of their workforce to the work-flow, and enabling employees to continue with home commitments (e.g. child care) and increased leisure activities.

KEEPING UP AND LOOKING AHEAD

The way to make sure you remain a marketable commodity in the rapidly changing workplace is to keep looking forward. If you're already in the work force and are looking to make a change, consider going back to school enrolling in a vocational programme. If you're still in school and are trying to choose a career, try to match your interests with the direction in which you see technology progressing.

Can you imagine our world without the technologies we take for granted. What if you, like Rip Van Winkle, fell asleep under a tree one bright sunny day at the turn of the century? Only you slept for more than 20 years – you slept for almost a hundred. Think of all the changes you'd see around you when you awoke: electricity, telephones, cars and airplanes – not to mention television, computers and rockets to the moon! All in less than 100 years!

Today more than ever, choosing an occupation is a risky business. Many jobs have disappeared when technology rendered them obsolete. A graphic illustration of this occurred not long ago in the newspaper industry. Linotype machines, which used hot type formed from molten lead, were the workhorses of almost every large newspaper in the country until the 1970s. Linotype operators were vital to these newspapers. By the 1980s however, cold type (set by computers) became standard in the newspaper industry. Linotype operator was an obsolete occupation within a decade.

That doesn't mean all of these people remained unemployed or unemployable. It means they had to learn new skills to keep up with advancing technology. Some operators were retrained to run the computers that set cold type.

It's impossible to predict the exact impact of each new technology. Scientific progress also depends on social, political and cultural attitudes. Even an invention as important as the telephone took more than 50 years to be widely accepted. Yet within a single decade of their invention, a majority of Americans had television in their homes.

All we can say for sure is that as we move toward a new century, technological advances will continue to change the way we live and work. The more you know about the world in which you live, the more effective will be your campaign to sell and market yourself.

20

DECIDING ON A MARKET
And Selling Yourself Effectively

'You increase the odds of making a sale by knowing what
the buying public wants and needs'

I presume that you're reading this book for one of two reasons: because
you're just starting out in life (career-wise), or because you're dissatisfied with your present situation and feel it's time to make a change. Either
way, it's your future we're talking about.

In the 60s, money took a back seat to the meaning and relevance of
work in the Hippie generation. In the 80s the Yuppies turned the pursuit
of wealth and power into an obsession. In the 90s, a healthier, more bal-
anced viewpoint of life and work is emerging. We're less willing to sacri-
fice everything for money but we do want to be paid well for what we do
well. We want jobs that will give us satisfaction, time to pursue other
important interests, and time to be with our family and friends.

It's in your best interest to pursue a line of work that gives you a good
sense of yourself along with a good salary. Using the principles of sales
and marketing we've discussed so far, and the specific selling tools you'll
discover in Part Five, you'll find it is possible to do satisfying work, and
be well paid for it.

STUDY THE MARKET

One way to shorten the job search process is to make a thorough study of
what's out there before you begin your marketing plan.

This means researching the industries and occupations that will give
you what you're looking for – career satisfaction, growth opportunities,
and commensurate salaries. By studying the market, you can make

decisions about how your interests and abilities fit into the best career opportunities.

The more specific your field of interest, the faster you can usually find employment. For example, if you go to law school and specialise in admiralty law or insurance law, you'll probably find a job before your classmate who's goal is to be a general solicitor. When your interests and background are more specialised, it's easier to focus your job search. If your interests are more general, or if you're changing from one field to another, it may take you longer to find the job of your choice.

30 JOBS WITH A FUTURE

The following list of 30 'hot' jobs is intended to give you an idea of how to match your interests and abilities to various growing occupations. The list includes a brief description of the occupation followed by the Success Factors you'll need to emphasise in order to sell yourself most effectively to employers in each field.

The jobs have been chosen because they are areas in which demand for employees is growing and is expected to continue doing so.

Don't be concerned if your area of interest isn't included in this list; you don't have to go after one of these jobs to be successful. You can apply the sales and marketing principles to *any* career you choose to pursue. Just be sure to do your homework: research the requirements of the field, the training you'll need and the best way to market yourself to the employer.

In addition to researching the overall market, you'll need to investigate specific companies. You want to work for people you trust and respect, in a company that treats its employees the same way.

Account Executives, Media Planners and Buyers, and Copy Writers

Advertising agencies are employed by companies to put together an advertising campaign for their product or service. Account executives are the contact between client and agent. They are involved in designing a suitable campaign within an allotted budget. Media planners and buyers decide on the best medium to use – for example TV, radio, magazines or bill boards – and are responsible for buying the advertising space or slot. Copy writers write copy for advertisements, product labels and packaging.

How to sell yourself: For all careers in advertising you will need to emphasise good communication and evaluation skills and you'll need to be a team player. Account executives and copy writers should be highly creative. Account executives in particular should market their decision-making skills.

Accountants and Auditors

Accountants prepare and analyse financial reports for many different purposes. They may specialise in such areas as taxes, budgeting or control. Auditors review a client's financial records and reports to judge their reliability.

How to sell yourself: If you have an aptitude for mathematics, are a stickler for detail and are able to compare, analyse and interpret facts and figures quickly you'll enjoy being an accountant. Sell your adaptability (you'll have to go from client to client); your independence (you'll often be working on your own); your responsibility (you'll be working with limited supervision); your reliability and integrity.

Actuary

Actuaries assemble and analyse insurance statistics to calculate probabilities of death, sickness, injury, unemployment, retirement, disability, etc. This information is then used to anticipate insurance losses. They design insurance and pension plans and make sure they are maintained on a sound financial basis.

How to sell yourself: People who love statistics are perfect for this job, which can be very lucrative. A strong aptitude for maths is essential. Your strongest selling point will be your evaluation skills, as you'll be called upon to integrate and analyse information from many different sources. Decision-making and foresight (the ability to project the results of your decisions) are also important.

Architect, Landscape Architect

An architect designs buildings and public areas. A landscape architect designs and plans landscaping for parks, golf courses, recreational areas, building sites, etc. Employment in this field is increasing due to the need to refurbish existing sites, and to growing budgets for city planning and historical preservation.

How to sell yourself: The best architects combine mathematical ability and a flair for solving technical problems with their artistic sensibilities. If you can easily visualise spatial relationships, this is a good field for you.

Develop your AAAs to emphasise your creativity and communications skills. And don't forget the team player Success Factor – architects usually work in teams.

Cashier

Handles payments from customers in supermarkets, department stores, cinemas, restaurants, etc.

How to sell yourself: This one of those occupations that's suffering from the decline in population growth and the aging of the workforce. Employers are searching for entry level people with a sense of commitment to their work (for many people, this will be their first job; it's also a good opportunity for retired older people). Sell your reliability, responsibility and honesty, and your ability to relate well to customers.

Chefs, Cooks and Kitchen Workers

People in these fields prepare meals that are tasty and attractively presented. There are opportunities for institutional chefs, cooks and kitchen workers, restaurant chefs and cooks, bread and pastry bakers, short order cooks and fast food cooks.

How to sell yourself: Besides needing a keen sense of smell and taste, you'll do well to market your creativity in this field. Another important Success Factor is team player. A pastry chef, for example, has to work with the head chef and the rest of the staff. A kitchen staff can be a close knit group, so this is a sought-after quality in this field. Chefs also need managerial, recruiting and supervisory skills, the ability to work well under pressure, and a readiness to adapt to changing and unorthodox schedules.

Chiropractors

Chiropractors practise a system of treatment based on the principle that a person's health is determined largely by the nervous system. They use 'manipulation' of the spine to alleviate pain, relieve pressure and reduce tension in the nervous system.

How to sell yourself: Chiropractors, like everyone in a health field, need a strong sense of commitment and a desire to help people. The most saleable skills include energy and enthusiasm, office organisation, independence, responsibility, and excellent public relations skills.

Computer Operator, Computer Programmer, Service Technician, Systems Analyst

Computers are now used in almost every conceivable business situation – stores, banks, colleges, government agencies, hospitals, factories, etc. Their usefulness depends on the skill of the people who run them. Computer programming is one of the fastest growing occupations. Programmers write detailed instructions (called programmes or software) that list in logical order the steps the computer must follow to organise data, solve a problem or do an assigned task. Computer systems analysts plan and develop methods for computerising business and scientific tasks or for improving computer systems already in use. Technicians are responsible for keeping intricate computer systems in good working order and repairing faulty systems. Technicians usually have several different clients, and go from job to job. They must be familiar with technical manuals and diagnostic programmes for each piece of equipment.

How to sell yourself: All computer fields are 'hot' now, but that means they're also competitive. To market yourself effectively, sell potential employers on your ability to think logically and analytically, your reliability, your problem-solving and decision-making skills, your oral and written communications skills, and your ability to work independently.

Dentist

Dentists diagnose and treat problems of the teeth and gums.

How to sell yourself: Dentists need manual dexterity and strong diagnostic abilities. Many dentists open private practices where the ability to work independently is essential. If you're looking to join an established practice, however, market your commitment, managerial, recruiting, and communications skills, reliability and your team player Success Factors.

Dental Assistant, Dental Hygienist

Assistants work at the chairside as dentists examine patients. They perform clerical and some laboratory duties. Hygienists provide preventative dental care, promote oral hygiene, and may develop and promote community dental health programmes.

How to sell yourself: Communications skills and your ability to follow instructions will be your strongest selling points for dental assistant positions. You also need to be a team player as you work closely with the dentist and office staff. Besides technical skills, hygienists should have an interest and background in biology, chemistry, health and psychology. Hygienists also need excellent communications skills, along with sales and marketing abilities (hygienists can contribute greatly to the expansion of a dentist's practice), as well as independence and reliability.

Dieticians and Nutritionists

These are professionals trained in applying principles of nutrition to food selection and meal preparation. They counsel individuals and groups, set up and supervise institutional food systems, and promote sound eating habits through education and research.

How to sell yourself: Being a team player will be one of your most marketable skills. You will also need organisational and administrative abilities. Increase your marketability by using your AAAs to demonstrate decision-making and evaluation abilities.

Employment Interviewer

Employment interviewers help job seekers find employment and help employers find qualified staff. Most new jobs in this area will be with temporary help or personnel consulting firms.

How to sell yourself: For this kind of job you need excellent communications and people skills. Market your adaptability (to work with a variety of clients), reliability, and evaluation skills.

Engineers (Civil, Metallurgic, Ceramic and Materials)

Civil engineers design and supervise construction of roads, airports, tunnels, bridges, water supply and sewage systems. Metallurgic, ceramic and materials engineers develop new types of metals and other materials tailored to meet specific requirements (for example, metals that are lightweight and heat resistant). Engineers will be needed to develop new materials and alloys and to adapt current ones to new applications.

How to sell yourself: Technical ability is important here; you need mathematical skills, mechanical drawing skills, precision and accuracy; you'll also need foresight, good communications skills, decision-making, team player and problem-solving capabilities.

Engineering Technicians

Engineering technicians assist engineers and scientists in research and development, preparing specifications, running tests, and studying ways to improve efficiency.

How to sell yourself: This is an exciting field for people who don't have or don't want the formal education and training necessary to be an engineer. You need an aptitude for maths and science. And since you'll have to work well with others, you'll need to market your team-player Success Factor, your oral and written communications skills, and your reliability.

Financial Services Managers

Practically every type of company has a financial manager: a treasurer, controller, or cash manager, who prepares financial reports required by the firm to conduct its operations and to satisfy tax and regulatory requirements. This broad category also includes careers in commercial and investment banking, personal credit institutions and other financial services industries.

How to sell yourself: Financial institutions look for people who are bright and well-rounded. They look for leadership qualities as well as decision-making skills, independence, oral and written communications skills, good judgment, and managerial talent.

Health Service Managers

The demand for good managers at health service organisations is expected to grow rapidly as the baby boomers age and force health care facilities and services to expand. Hospitals will provide some jobs, with others expected to be in medical group practices, nursing homes, etc.

How to sell yourself: For any job in the health services field it's essential that you enjoy working with people and have good communications skills. You'll also need to sell your sense of commitment, responsibility, decision-making and managing abilities, recruiting and staffing skills; you may also need public speaking skills.

Hotel Managers and Assistants

Hotal managers and assistants are responsible for the efficiency and profitable operation of their establishments. These are general and assistant positions as well as more specific managerial positions, e.g.

restaurant, catering, reservations, housekeeping, conventions, and customer services managers.

How to sell yourself: Adaptability is a key Success Factor necessary for this kind of career. Your AAAs should demonstrate your ability to get along with a variety of customers and staff, as well as your ability to handle stress. Market your decision-making, problem-solving and customer service skills as well as your reliability, responsibility and organisational abilities.

Human Services Counsellors

These are paraprofessionals working in correctional institutions, community mental health centres, family conciliation centres, RELATE (formerly Marriage Guidance Counsel), and drug abuse and alcoholism centres.

How to sell yourself: You'll need a background in social work or behavioural science for this career choice. Your selling points are your commitment and desire to help others. Patience, understanding and a caring nature are also necessary. A cheerful, up-beat personality is a definite plus. Good communications skills, and a strong sense of responsibility are other highly marketable qualities in this field.

Lawyers

This term covers two main professions: solicitors and barristers. Solicitors deal directly with the public offering legal advice and services. Barristers represent the client in court after being approached through a solicitor. There are many kinds of law specialities to be considered, such as corporate law, property law, divorce law, environmental law, tax law, etc. Legal assistants or 'paralegals' are less qualified than barristers and solicitors and offer less specialised advice.

How to sell yourself: Being a lawyer is not always as exciting or glamorous as it appears on TV, but the law can be a very interesting and satisfying career choice. You need integrity, honesty, and the ability to work with others. Selling points are decision-making and problem-solving skills, foresight, independence, and excellent communications skills.

Legal Assistants

Legal assistants help lawyers investigate facts and gather information about legal precedents and judicial decisions. You may also be asked to assist at trials or help draft legal documents.

How to sell yourself: This is another exciting and interesting career choice – but there is also a lot of legwork and drudgery involved, especially at entry level. Market yourself as reliable and responsible, full of initiative and creativity, and as someone with excellent decision-making, problem solving and communications skills.

Marketing Executives, Market Researchers

Of course you know by now that marketing entails all the activities involved in getting a product or service from the seller to the buyer. Market researchers are involved in research into who buys what, when, where and how.

How to sell yourself: For careers in all areas of marketing your AAAs should reflect a heavy emphasis on communications skills, creativity, evaluation, decision-making and foresight.

Management Analysts and Consultants

Management analysts and consultants are called in to solve organisational problems, to collect, review and analyse data, make recommendations and assist in implementation of their proposals.

How to sell yourself: Many analysts and consultants work on their own and are their own small businesses. Larger consulting firms have a staff of several consultants, each an expert in a different area. You must have strong interpersonal skills and be able to work on a variety of projects at once. Excellent probing and questioning skills and a customer-service orientation will be your best selling points, along with evaluation, decision-making and problem-solving skills, foresight, independence and creativity.

Property Managers

Property managers control income-producing commercial and residential properties, and community associations. They may also plan and direct the purchase, development and disposal of property for businesses. Or they may be involved in the day-to-day management of property for owners. A large portion of new jobs in this area will be in office and retail space, as well as rental housing.

How to sell yourself: If you're going to market yourself in this field, you'll have to demonstrate your decision-making and problem-solving abilities, and that you are responsible and have excellent communications skills.

Public Relations Executives

PR executives help businesses, governments, hospitals, universities, and other organisations to build and maintain positive relationships with the public.

How to sell yourself: You need an outgoing personality and excellent communications skills for this career choice. Many PR professionals start their own business, others join a public relations firm, or work in the PR department of a large company (this is where the highest paying jobs are located). Selling points are persistence, rapport building skills, creativity, enthusiasm, adaptability, initiative and an ability to function well as part of a team.

Physiotherapists

Physiotherapists help the disabled or injured to become physically functional. It may involve stretching and manipulating the patient's arms and legs, using exercise equipment, and working closely with a medical team.

How to sell yourself: Develop your AAAs to emphasise your sense of commitment and responsibility. Also your team player skills, as well as your ability to relate and explain procedures to patients. Decision-making and evaluation skills would also be a strong selling point for a career in physiotherapy.

Receptionists

Every business wants to make a good first impression. The receptionist plays a key role in that area, which is why this job will always be in demand. Duties vary, but most receptionists greet customers and visitors, determine their needs, and refer the caller to the person who can help them.

How to sell yourself: One of your most effective marketing tools in this field is your appearance. Since you're the first person visitors and clients may see, how you look is vital to the company. Sell your other strong points, such as communications skills (especially your telephone voice and manners), your customer service orientation, and your reliability.

Retail Sales and Service Sales Personnel

The job of a retail salesperson is to sell merchandise to customers. Service sales representatives sell a wide variety of services, from linen supplies to cable TV to telephone communications systems. They also sell services such as payroll processing, temporary help, consulting, advertising, etc.

How to sell yourself: Retail sales will provide more job openings than almost any other occupation through the year 2000. This field is especially appealing for part-time and temporary workers. To market yourself effectively for these positions, you need to be energetic, reliable and independent with strong communications skills. You also need the ability to work under pressure.

Teachers

Teaching involves imparting knowledge to others. The pupils may be children in private or state run schools, students in colleges and universities, or adults in adult education centres.

How to sell yourself: You'll need dedication and commitment for a career in teaching, as well as excellent communications skills. You'll also need to market your supervisory skills and the ability to evaluate the performance and progress of your pupils. School teachers will need masses of energy. Clear thinking and creativity will be added selling points.

Writers and Editors

This career involves communications through the written and spoken word. Writers develop original fiction and non-fiction for books, magazines, trade journals, newspapers, technical manuals and studies, radio, film, TV and advertising. Editors supervise writers and select and prepare material for publication or broadcast.

How to sell yourself: Writing and editing are both highly competitive fields. Many people do it on a freelance basis. The fastest growing areas for writers and editors are the technical fields. With the increasing complexity of industrial and scientific equipment and inventions, there is a high demand for people with a talent for writing and editing simple explanations and instructions. To market yourself in this field you'll have to demonstrate your communications skills and emphasise your reliability, creativity, independence and commitment to getting a job done on deadline.

PART FIVE

CLOSING THE SALE

21

SALES TECHNIQUES:
How to Use Sales Basics to Get the Job of Your Choice

'The art of closing a sale is the ability to sell to the
right person in the right way at the right time'

A sale isn't a single action or a straight line from beginning to end. It's a complex operation made up of many smaller components.

Each component is vitally important to the process as a whole. You might be tempted to skip one or two of the steps and go right to 'Closing the Sale.' It won't work. You'll be wondering why you're not getting the job offers you want. You can't construct a building on a shaky foundation, and you can't get the job you want without going through all the necessary steps.

This chapter is an Introductory Course on the Basics of Sales, intended to acquaint you with the *key* elements of the sales process. The chapters that follow will expand on these techniques, and show you how each of them is applied to your personal marketing effort.

These are the five parts of the sale that make up the foundation for your job search effort:

- Prospecting
- Building Report
- Qualifying
- Handling Objections
- Closing the Sale

PROSPECTING: THE SEARCH FOR POTENTIAL CUSTOMERS

The term prospect applies to anyone who is a potential customer for your product or service. Before you begin your sales effort (or in this case, your job search), you need to have a rough idea of whose those prospective customers (or potential employers) might be.

Prospecting begins with the *lead*. A lead is nothing more than a piece of information that directs you to a person or company where someone is likely to see you or speak to you.

Once you start talking to a live person, you've got yourself a prospect.

Picture your ideal prospect

Does every employer in the world represent a potential job for you? Not really. Just as in sales, where no one product or service is right for everyone, not every available job is right for you. You want to be selective with your time and energy. To find out what kinds of employers you should be actively seeking, paint a mental picture of your Ideal Prospect.

This is a picture of a person who:

1. Has the need for your particular talents and abilities.
2. Has the necessary budget to meet your salary requirements.
3. Has the authority to make the hiring decision.

In my business as a speaker, for example, my Ideal Prospect would be someone who is planning a meeting for next month and must find a speaker immediately, who has read one of my books and/or seen me speak, who is looking for an expert in sales techniques, who has the appropriate budget and the authority to sign a contract on the spot.

To picture your Ideal Prospect, ask yourself these questions:

- Does this prospective employer want or need what I have to offer?
- Does this prospective employer have the necessary budget?
- Does this prospective employer have the final say in who gets hired?

Of course, you will have other criteria that are particular to your individual job search. Your Ideal Prospect may have to be within a limited commuting distance, for instance, or be able to offer you work on a flexible schedule.

Keith is a young family man with two school-aged children. He's looking for a job on a newspaper so that he can work a flexible schedule and be at home after school while his wife is at work. His Ideal Prospect would be a publisher who's just lost his City Editor, needs someone who can work nights, and who has the authority to employ him.

There are very few real-life Ideal Prospects and you may have to compromise. But if your potential employers have no resemblance at all to the ideal, you're going to be wasting both your time and theirs.

Creative prospecting is a basic concept in planning your immediate job search or your long-term career strategy. The more potential employers you can reach, the more options you have. When it comes to prospecting, more is better. You would never expect to hit a home run every time you go to bat. The more times you get up and swing, the better your chances of hitting the ball. So it is with job offers. You can't expect to get a job offer every time you go to an interview, but the more interviews you go on, the more job offers you'll get.

Leading the way

It all starts with the lead. There are two basic types of leads: referred leads and non-referred leads. You get non-referred leads from sources such as newspaper, trade paper or magazine advertisements, and association or industry directories.

Remember, though, you're not just looking for the *most* leads, you're looking for the *best* leads. Keep your Ideal Prospect in mind and it will be easier to find leads that are likely to put you in touch with people who are interested in what you have to offer.

Referred leads come to you from another person. A referral can come from a prospect who doesn't employ you but knows someone else who might be interested. Or it can come from former employers, from acquaintances, friends or family – in fact from anyone who knows someone else. There's no way to predict who among your contacts will produce the best leads. Therefore you should ask everyone you speak to for referrals.

If a referral doesn't work out, ask *that* person for a referral. Keep the chain going so you always have another lead to follow. Use the networking notebook set up in your marketing plan.

That's what Theo did. Theo came to my 'How to Market Yourself' seminar as a newcomer to New York City. Divorced and with two grown children, Theo had moved to the city with a few personal belongings, a computer, a lot of determination and a well-worn tape of Frank Sinatra singing 'New York, New York'. Like Frank, Theo believed that if 'you can make it here, you can make it anywhere'. He knew very few people here however, and none in his chosen field of desktop publishing. He had been a chemistry teacher for 20 years, but was determined to make a successful career change.

Through a friend, he heard of a Special Interest Group (or SIG as these groups are called) for Apple Macintosh users and went to check it out. He met many people who had similar interests to his, and continued to attend meetings and swap ideas with other members. A few weeks later, when the group needed a new art director for its monthly newsletter (a non-paying, volunteer position), several people suggested Theo. Theo accepted the job and worked very hard to make it a success. SIG members were so impressed by his talent and his diligence, they began referring him to clients and to other desktop publishers who needed extra help. Within three months, Theo was offered a full time position at a well known advertising firm.

As we discussed in Chapter 18 (Your Marketing Plan), networking is your most important marketing tool. It's the basis for the old saying, 'It's not what you know, it's who you know that counts.' Anyone can be 'well-connected'. The numbers are staggering – your network consists of the number of people you know, plus the number of people they know, plus the number of people *they* know, and so on. With these kinds of numbers behind you, how can you lose?

Adventures in networking

Perhaps the most valuable asset of networking is that it is by nature an *active* process. It helps you to help yourself; nobody else can network for you. Has this ever happened to you: a friend says, 'Oh, I met someone yesterday who has a widget manufacturing company. I know you've always been interested in widgets, so I told him about you. Here's his number. He said to give him a call.'? What is your reaction? Do you pick up the phone immediately? Or do you think, 'Well, I'll call next week,' or 'I'll call when I have more time,' or 'I'll call when I get my life together'? Or do you think the man was just being polite and would only be annoyed if you called?

If your reaction is not to call, think again. If you are sincerely interested in widgets, chances are this person would be happy to speak with you. He may not be able to help you advance in your career or offer you a new job, but you may find out some fascinating facts about widgets.

Networking is an adventure. You never know where it will lead. My staff always kid me, because I'm constantly networking – sometimes in unlikely places. Every time I travel I make friends with the people sitting next to me. I've received consulting assignments from several people, sold products and learned many new and interesting facts about my business and theirs. I've networked in department stores, while getting a manicure, and during intermission at the theatre. I never let an opportunity slip by – follow up on every lead you get and you never know what surprises life has in store for you!

BUILDING RAPPORT: THE GOLDEN RULE OF SELLING

Building rapport is one of the most important steps in the sales process, because *people buy from people they like, trust and respect.*

People like you when you're on the same wavelength as they are – when they feel you're concerned about their needs as well as your own.

People trust you when you're forthright and honest – when you're up front and confident about who you are and what your goals are.

People respect you when you treat them with respect. People sense a bad attitude a mile away. The Golden Rule applies to everyone, including prospective employers.

My husband was once interviewing candidates for a new secretarial position in his office. Sheila arrived 15 minutes late for her appointment. She rushed in without apology, said, 'Hi. I'm Sheila,' and stuffed her CV into my husband's hand. She answered his questions crisply and abruptly, repeatedly pointing to the sheet of paper she'd thrust at my husband and saying, 'It's all on my CV.'

Sheila had come highly recommended and her qualifications were perfect. But her attitude was not. 'She acted as if I were imposing on her by asking questions,' my husband told me. 'I knew right away that she was able to do the job. I also knew immediately that she wouldn't fit in with the rest of the team.'

Your first contact with a potential employer, whether it's through a letter, a telephone conversation or face-to-face meetings, can determine your success or failure to close the sale. 'You can never go back and re-meet someone for the first time,' says Joe Gandolpho, the world's largest seller of insurance and number one financial and estate planner. 'A successful salesperson knows how important first impressions are in sales.'

The purpose of this first contact is to establish a positive business relationship. Once that is accomplished, you can move ahead with the next step of the sales process.

QUALIFYING: SELLING TO THE RIGHT PERSON

Would you try to sell eyeglasses to a person with 20/20 vision? No matter how good a salesperson you are, a person with perfect sight won't need your product. You can waste a lot of time pursuing fruitless leads. A prospect is 'qualified' when he or she has the need or desire for what you have to offer, has the necessary budget, and has the authority to buy – when he or she closely matches the picture of your Ideal Prospect.

How do you know if a buyer is qualified? You have to do preliminary research and ask questions to find out how well this buyer measures up to your Ideal. Sales trainer Tom Hopkins estimates that a sale to a qualified prospect can be closed 50% of the time, while unqualified ones will buy only 10% of the time. The more you know about a potential customer, the more likely your chances of making the sale. By selling to qualified leads, you cut your sales effort in half and multiply your chances of closing the sale by a factor of five.

HANDLING OBJECTIONS: TURNING 'NO' INTO 'YES'

An objection is what you hear when a buyer hasn't yet made a positive decision. The most important lesson a salesperson can learn, however, is that an objection is not equal to a rejection. It's a very rare sale that goes along smoothly from beginning to end.

You're with a customer who's very interested in purchasing the camera you're selling. But when you mention the price, the customer says, 'Sorry. I don't have the money right now.' You could just say, 'Oh. I'm sorry to hear that,' and lose the sale. Or you could say, 'If you had the money, would you buy the camera?' When the customer says yes, you could then work out a time-payment plan, or some other mutually beneficial arrangement.

Remember this: an objection is simply a request for more information. If at a job interview an interviewer says he's looking for someone who's had a little more experience in the field, you can let him know about related experience you have and how your enthusiasm for learning new skills will more than make up for what you lack.

Objections are usually perceived as roadblocks to a sale. The truth is that objections are the gateways to moving a sale forward. Do you know why canned or memorised sales pitches don't work? Because the prospect doesn't get a chance to object.

Now you may be thinking, 'I don't want the prospect to object. If the prospect objects, that means he doesn't want to employ me.' But all he did was object. When prospects raise objections, they are offering you the reasons they can't make a yes decision right now. When someone tells you 'the price is too high,' it means the terms of the sale, *the way they currently understand them*, are not yet acceptable. There has been some miscommunication somewhere along the line.

Once that objection is voiced, you have the opportunity to clear up the misunderstanding. An objection isn't a rejection, it's a question or concern that hasn't been answered yet.

If the prospect doesn't ask any questions or raise any objections, it could be a sign that she's simply not interested. She may not realise that you have a variety of skills that will meet her needs. So you should welcome the chance to handle the objection. It's another chance to sell yourself. I'll go into detail about handling objections in Chapter 26.

CLOSING THE SALE: REMEMBERING YOUR ABCs

When a sale is closed, it means that the buyer has come to a favourable decision. Every salesperson's ultimate goal is to close the sale so that all parties benefit. The salesperson gets rewarded financially, and the buyer finds a solution to a problem.

In order to close the sale, you have to do three things: show the customer why purchasing your product will be of benefit to him; handle any objections that may arise; and ask for the order.

Our camera salesman, presented with the objection that the customer 'doesn't have the money right now,' asked a trial closing question. 'If you had the money, would you buy the camera?' The customer said yes. Then the salesperson went on to say, 'If I can show you how you can pay for this camera on an easy instalment plan, would that be of interest to you?' Again, the customer said yes. All along, the salesperson used his ABCs: Always Be Closing.

Remembering your ABCs is an important lesson to learn. Throughout your marketing effort, you'll be using these sales techniques to present yourself to qualified buyers. You'll use these skills to show potential employers how hiring you can fill their needs, answer any objections, and confidently 'ask for the order.' If the interview has gone well and you think this is a job you would like, don't walk out with just a smile and a handshake. You want to be offered the job, even if you ultimately decide not to take it. Your interview should end with a closing question, such as 'I'm very interested in working with you and your company. Can I call you tomorrow at noon to get your answer?'

22

THE DIRECT MAIL APPROACH:
How to Make an Irresistible Offer

'The secret desire of every prospective buyer is, "make me
an offer I can't refuse"'

'**Y**ou may have already won a million pounds!'
Have you ever received such a note? It's a direct mail letter. So are most of the letters you get from charities, magazine publishers, timeshare companies and mail order companies. Thousands of businesses, large and small, are taking advantage of what is proving to be one of the most effective marketing tools around – direct mail.

You too can take advantage of this very successful marketing tool. More and more small business owners are choosing the direct mail approach as the most effective and economical means of getting their product known.

Where your job search is concerned, you have to have some way of letting people know you're around. How will you go about it? Radio? TV? Newspapers? Direct mail?

Radio and television are much too expensive to be practical 'advertising' choices. Most newspapers have a column called 'Situations Wanted', where people seeking employment place ads. Nine out of ten employers I asked said they very rarely thought of looking there.

Financial considerations aside, radio, TV and newspapers aren't useful marketing tools for you because you have no idea of who your 'audience' will be. You may be reaching millions of uninterested people.

That's why direct mail is so effective. Because it gives you a chance to reach a very specific group of potential buyers – buyers you already know have an interest in what you have to sell. When you created your Marketing Plan in Chapter 18, you came up with a list of specific individuals to contact. Your job now is to convince them that it is in their interests to employ you. This process begins with your introductory letter – the direct mail piece.

In order to create an irresistible mailing piece, familiarise yourself with the concept of Marketing by Specific Objective. The clearer your understanding of each phase of your marketing campaign, the more effective it will be. You have to know the exact purpose of your letter, or you'll have a hard time knowing what to include.

YOUR FIRST OBJECTIVE:
BAITING THE HOOK

What is the objective of the letter? When I ask this question at seminars, the usual answers are, 'to get a job' or 'to get an interview'. That may be your eventual goal, but the specific objective of the letter is to arouse your prospective employer's interest enough so that when you call, he or she will want to talk to you. That's all the letter needs to do. It is bait.

Your goal at this step of your marketing strategy is to pique someone's interest – to convince this person that you are someone worth seeing. You want this letter to put you at the top of the potential candidate list. The only way you can accomplish this is by getting the right letter to the right person.

THE ONE–TWO MARKETING PUNCH:
THE LIST AND THE OFFER

The secret of success in direct mail marketing is the combination of the list and the offer. The list consists of the people you have targeted to receive your mailing. A good, well-researched list provides you with a group of customers who have reasons to be interested in what you're trying to sell. If you send a mediocre letter to the right list, you still have a fair chance of success. But even a great letter sent to the wrong list won't get you anywhere. It's like offering a vegetarian a juicy steak dinner. No matter how beautifully cooked, the vegetarian won't be interested. Last week I got a mail shot from a publication called *Golf Magazine*. I don't play golf. I don't like golf. I'm sure it's a wonderful sport, and a good magazine – but it's of no interest to me. I was on the wrong list.

No single product, service or person appeals to everyone. That's why Ford makes saloons, estate cars and sports cars. Only a very specific group of people will be interested in you – and the more specific the group, the more they'll be interested. For instance, if you were seeking a job as a researcher in an oil company, the type of person who would be *most* interested in you would be a head researcher who has just lost two of his three best people and is in a rush to meet a deadline. The type of person who would be least interested would be a head researcher who is overstaffed and has no new projects on the horizon.

You made up your list in the Immediate Action Plan section of your marketing plan. You now have a list of 10 or 20 individual names of companies where you'll be seeking employment. This is what's known as a *targeted list* – it's not just a random sampling of names, but a carefully considered group of people who all have an interest in the product or service you have to 'sell'. These are *hot prospects*!

The offer is the interest-getter. It's the answer to the customer's question, 'What's in it for me?' It might be a 'low, low discounted price'. Or 'buy one, get one free,' or 'subscribe now and get this stylish pen and pencil set'. It's your proposition to the client or customer: 'Use my service and . . .' or 'buy my product and . . .'.

The offer to your 'buyer' is that you will do for him what you have done for others – 'Employ me and I'll solve your distribution problem . . .' or 'Make me a part of your team and I'll increase your productivity . . .'. One or two of your most relevant accomplishments, presented in terms of clearly applicable benefits to the reader, will often make the prospective employer want to see you even if there is no immediate job opening.

Carol, an experienced legal assistant specialising in tax law, lived and worked in London for 12 years. When her husband was transferred to Birmingham, she began to look for work there. She wanted to remain in tax law. Cara wrote a well thought out, benefit-oriented direct-mail letter. She didn't target her list, however, and sent the letter to dozens of solicitors' firms that had no tax departments. Once she realised that she wasn't getting the response she'd hoped for, Carol went back to her list, and targeted it at 20 tax lawyers in the Birmingham area.

She was able to set up 5 interviews within a two-week period, and eventually was offered three different jobs. By sending the right letter to the right people, Carol ended up having her choice of several offers.

PERSONALISE YOUR OFFER

It might be easier to send out one mass mailing (using exactly the same letter) to all the people on your list. But a good direct mail letter makes the reader feel special for having received it, as if the person who wrote the letter took the time and effort to get to know something about him (which is what you have done). In this way, direct mail gets the reader emotionally involved with the sale (remember: 'people buy for emotional reasons'). In fact, a primary value of personalised direct mail is that it allows you to appeal both to the business (or intellectual) and personal (or emotional) sides of the 'buyer' at one time.

Suppose you run a fence repair service. You pass a beautiful house surrounded by a lovely white picket fence. You notice that one section is beginning to fall over, and the paint is starting to peel. How effective a salesperson would you be if you mailed that homeowner one of your standard brochures:

> DEAR HOMEOWNER:
> DON'T DESPAIR OVER DISREPAIR
> WE REPAIR WITH LOVING CARE.
> FOR QUALITY SERVICE CALL
> SHERRI SMITH, FENCEMENDERS

You might get a response. The homeowner might call, but more likely he'd throw it on the pile with all the other junk mail.

But what if you wrote a letter like this:

Dear Jones Family,

As I walked by your beautiful home the other day, I noticed that your white picket fence was just beginning to need looking after. I've been in the fence-mending business for 20 years, and I know how to make your fence sturdy, bright and beautiful once again.

Just ask the Bradley family down the street. The value of their house increased by 1/3 because of the fence work we did on their property. And if we start work on your fence before October 30th, we'll repair your driveway at no additional cost.

I'll call you next week to see how I may be of service.

Sincerely,

Sherri Smith
Fencemenders

This letter has obviously been sent specifically to the Jones family and not to a hundred anonymous homeowners. Mr Jones can't help but feel that if you took the time and effort to write him a personal letter, you would also take time and effort to fix his fence. The letter was targeted, the offer irresistible. Mr Jones may still have several questions to ask you – he isn't necessarily going to hire you on the spot – but in all likelihood he will speak with you when you call. And that's all your letter was intended to do.

Writing successful direct mail copy is a branch of the advertising industry that is just now coming into full bloom. In his book *Guerilla Marketing – Secrets for Making Big Profits from Your Small Business*, Jay

Conrad Levinson says, 'Direct Marketing is growing faster than any other type of marketing. More and more people trust it . . .' It stands to reason then, that in creating a marketing strategy that is part of a lifelong career plan, we should utilise direct mail – the major marketing method of the future.

Finally, creating an effective direct mail letter is a skill that must be learned and practised. Don't send your first efforts to the people you'd most like to work for. Have friends or family look at the letter and ask them if they would want to see you. Have them explain why or why not. Then send your letter to someone at the bottom of your list of prospective employers. Do your practising with the jobs that appeal to you least and by the time you get to your top choices, you'll be a professional.

ATTENTION TO DETAIL

First and foremost, a direct mail piece is a personal letter, so be sure you have the right person. You want to reach the decision maker, the person who has direct responsibility for employing you. So if you're contacting a fairly small company, you would write directly to the managing director. For a large organisation, you would go to the head of the relevant department.

Be sure you have the *correct spelling* and *proper title*. It's always best to call and make sure the person is still there, and that their title hasn't changed.

You don't have to identify yourself when you call. You can simply say, 'I'm sending some information to Mr Tompkins, and I'd like to have the correct spelling of his full name and his full title.' Once again, this shows a sense of caring and attention to detail that may be taken for granted if all is in order – but will surely be noticed and held against you if you make an error.

'Have I got a proposition for you . . . ?'

Now that you know who you're writing to, you want to make a business proposition: you will apply your knowledge, experience, expertise and energy toward solving this individual's (and this company's) problems. In return you'll receive a salary, benefits, and job satisfaction. You're not pleading for the job out of desperation, nor demanding the position because you feel you deserve it; you're suggesting a mutually beneficial arrangement. You know the benefits to you. Your letter must demonstrate the benefits to the other party.

Your opening paragraph has three objectives:

1. To gain attention.
2. To refer specifically to the needs of the person and the organisation to whom you are writing.
3. To establish the value of the product (you).

Your research should have told you something about the successes and failures, the strengths and weaknesses of the companies you are contacting. Here's the opportunity to use what you've learned. You should at least know the special interests of this organisation, so that you can point out just how hiring you would solve a problem or further an interest.

Take, for example, the letter from Fencemenders to the Jones family. It begins: 'As I walked by your beautiful home the other day, I noticed that your white picket fence was just beginning to need looking after.' This says (after complimenting the family's home) that Fencemenders is aware that a problem exists, and that they might be able to help. You don't necessarily have to point out the problem (no one likes to be told they're not doing a good job), but you do want to make it clear you know what is needed. You also want to make it clear that you are bottom-line oriented. Fencemenders included the statement about the Bradley family: 'The value of their house increased by ⅓ because of the fence work we did. . . .'

Your letter might include a statement like: 'Having had five years' experience as a Quality Control Analyst, I know I can reduce costs and increase production for you and your company.' This lets the individual know that your interests, and the company's, are the same.

Reduce the risk factor

You also want to substantiate your value by including samples of how your abilities have previously benefited others. Employers want to know what you've done for competitors and colleagues. The natural assumption is that if you've done something well for someone else, you can do so for them. You know that the hiring process is just as hard on prospective employers as it is on you; that employers are often taking a large risk, sometimes putting their careers on the line, when they take on someone new. If you can show that you have successfully solved problems for others, you reduce the risk factor.

So here you would include two (or at the most three) of your AAAs – carefully chosen and worded so that they are relevant to the needs of this particular company.

Would you respond to a letter like this:

August 9, 1990

Ms Rachael A. Miller
Happyface Health Care Ltd
Sullivan Street
London SW1

Dear Ms Miller,
    I am a research and design expert. My research has been in personal dental hygiene and my designs are very successful.
    Recently I was told that you have a job opening in your department. I'll be in London the first two weeks in September. If you have an interest in discussing our working together, please call me before then so that we can set up a meeting for that time.

Yours sincerely
Jack Washington

There's nothing in this letter that distinguishes Jack Washington from the crowd. Judging from this letter alone, Ms Miller wouldn't have any reason to call. It's not a terrible letter; it's just innocuous. That's just the trouble. I've received many letters like this. I never give them a second glance.

Just telling an employer you're an expert proves nothing. Why should she believe you, a total stranger? Jack didn't list any of his accomplishments, and he didn't bring up any benefits for the reader. And finally, he's leaving the next step up to the potential employer, asking her to call to set up an appointment. There isn't sufficient bait in this letter to get her to call.

DISSECTING A SUCCESSFUL LETTER

Now, let's go through the direct mail letter step by step:

1. Be sure to call the company and verify that the prospective employer is still there, the correct spelling of her name and her proper title.

2. Open with a statement about the reader. Let her know that this is a personal letter, not a mass mailing, and that you know something about her and/or the company. This paragraph should grab the reader's attention and convince her to go on reading even if there is no immediate job opening. It should imply that you are compatible with the company's aims and values – that you'll 'fit in' to the organisation, and to her department. It should make you stand out from the rest of the letter writers who haven't done their research as well.

Most introductory letters are formula and unimaginative. They don't say much more than 'I need a job. Please employ me. I'll wait for your call.' So if you send a well-written, carefully researched letter, you'll be well ahead of the game – and you'll be remembered.

3. *Give the reader a glimpse of your abilities.* Pique his or her curiosity, with a hint that hiring you will solve certain problems – increase profits, improve efficiency, generate creative ideas, etc. Focus on benefits. Let her know what line of work you are in, a general idea of your experience, and how you could apply that experience to her company. You don't necessarily have to state experience in number of years. You can use pound figures, or the number of fund raisers you have chaired, or projects you've completed, or any other number that would give an indication that your background is compatible to this company's immediate and future concerns.

4. *List two of your most relevant AAAs.* This is your irresistible offer. This is what makes someone sit up and take notice, and say to themselves, 'We could really use someone like that around here!' Make sure your accomplishments relate to this particular company's interests. Keep descriptions brief and to the point; you don't want to give everything away in the letter – you can always elaborate in the interview. Stress the results. It's not necessary to mention the name of the company for whom you achieved these results. Keep the employer on the hook. Also, you don't want someone to look at your letter and say, 'Oh, yeah, Acme. I know them. We don't do the same thing they do.' You don't want to give the employer the chance to make such a rash judgment. You can always be more specific and tell her the name of the company when you get to the interview.

5. *To close the letter, let the reader know what will happen next.* Set up a specific date on which you'll be calling to schedule an appointment. Use the word 'appointment' or 'meeting', or even 'a time to see you'; avoid using the word 'interview'. You're only asking for an opportunity to discuss business. If a job offer comes out of this meeting, so much the better. And write with confidence, as if you're expecting the meeting to take place. Write the date you say you will call in your diary and stick to it. If your letter is sufficiently intriguing, the reader will be very curious about you and will be waiting to hear from you. He or she will be expecting someone who actively pursues their goals; a person who has energy and initiative, not someone who is passively sitting by the phone waiting for a call.

6. *You might want to include a PS.* An inside secret of the direct mail industry says that people read the salutation first and any PS. next. A

PS. can be very effective and should include an additional incentive for the reader to speak with you when you call. They'll be waiting, or maybe even call you first. If you want to make a more formal first impression, put this information in the body of the letter and leave out the PS.

7. *Make a Good Impression* I was in a client's office once when he received a letter inquiring about a job opening. The letter was rumpled, torn and was obviously a copy. My client said, 'I don't care how skilled or talented this person is. I would never employ anyone who cared so little about the impression this letter would make. If he thinks I won't notice, he's wrong. I'm looking for a professional. No professional would send me a letter like this.'

Go over your letter and make sure it's perfectly and professionally typed. No typos or grammatical errors. Good quality paper, not ripped, torn or mutilated. Before posting your letter, take the following important steps:

- Copy the letter for your files.
- Note the date and the person to call in your diary.
- Write the phone number on your copy of the letter.
- File the copy of the letter in a clearly designated place.

The following is an example of a successful direct mail letter:

August 9, 1990

Ms Rachael A. Miller
Vice President, Research & Design
Happyface Health Care Ltd
Sullivan Street
London SW1

Dear Ms Miller,
Your new design innovations in tooth care products tell me you are interested in improving dental health as well as expanding your market. As a research and design expert with 10 years' experience in personal hygiene products, I am continually discovering new and better methods of personal health care, and I do so in practical, profitable ways.
— Last year I increased sales of my company's curved-handled toothbrushes 300% by designing an inexpensive plastic adapter that allowed these brushes to fit standard bathroom holders.
— My suggestion for, and subsequent design of, better packaging for my company's 'Little Brusher' children's toothpaste moved this product from a 2% share of the market to a 22% share in just six months.

I can bring the same kind of successes to you and your fine organisation. I will be in London the first two weeks in September. I'll call you on Tuesday, August 16th to set up a meeting for that time.

Yours sincerely
Jack Washington

PS. I was particularly impressed with your new floss dispenser, and would like to discuss a plan I've devised for a profitable line of coordinated products.

TIMING IS EVERYTHING

One final but important consideration in direct mail marketing is *when* to send the letter. You want to try and time the letter's arrival so that it will get the attention it deserves.

Call your local post office and find out how many days it will take your letter to reach its destination. The best time to post it is so that it arrives on a Tuesday or Wednesday. Monday is too heavy a mail day and it might get lost amongst so many items, and Friday is a day when many people are finishing things off and trying to leave early.

Your letter will be the first impression you make on a prospective employer. Make it a good one. This letter should be more than an introduction to one individual, it should be part of a lifetime plan of searching out opportunity. You are building connections with every letter and CV you send. Did I say CV? A CV wouldn't be my first choice connection-builder, but sometimes a CV is what's required. If you have to write a CV, the next chapter will show you the best way to do it.

23

HOW TO WRITE A CV

'In the age of customer service, mass marketing is not as effective as an individually customised sales approach'

When I was an actress 'making the rounds' and going out on auditions, I always had at least two sets of photographs with me. If I was auditioning for a more dramatic role, I would hand the director the looking straight-ahead, no-smile, dark background picture. If I was going for a comedy or a musical role, I'd use the brightly lit, shining-eyed, big-smile photograph. It wasn't that the director didn't have the imagination to see beyond my photograph – it's just that I needed all the help I could get.

At some point in his or her career, every actor or actress goes to a 'cattle call.' This is a pre-audition screening process where a director will usually line up 10 or 12 people in a room, take a quick look down the line, and tell most of the people to go home. They just aren't what he's looking for. It's got nothing to do with their talent or past experience. Once this quick weeding-out period is over, the real auditions begin.

Some wise actors and actresses have learned to increase their chances of making it past the first hurdle. Before they go to a cattle call, they do some research and find out as much as they can about the play, the film and/or the director. They then make small adjustments to their appearance – such as changing the way they dress, or combing their hair differently – make it easier for the director to picture them in the context of the play or movie.

ONE CV DOESN'T FIT ALL

Sending 'blind' CVs when you don't know anything about the job or the company – is the job market cattle call. Many employers will take a quick

174

glance down the line of CVs they receive and reject most of them. That's because most of the CVs they receive tell them very little about the people who send them, and nothing at all about why those people should be considered for this job.

That's why I don't like CVs. They are used to screen people out after only a cursory glance or two. That's also why the direct mail approach is a much better sales tool. In your letter, you're making a targeted offer with the benefits to the buyer clearly spelled out for him. CVs never have the same impact.

I would like to be able to tell you not to use a CV ever. In the real world, however, we have to deal with the way things are. Most employers will insist upon seeing one. When that happens, my advice is to study the 'role' and the 'director' carefully beforehand – find out as much about the job and employer as possible – and present the employer with an image of yourself tailored to his needs and expectations (a customised, which I'll explain later on in this chapter).

ATTRACTING ATTENTION: BREAK THE PREOCCUPATION

Like your direct mail letter, the CV is intended to attract attention, not to get you the job. It's purpose is to get your foot in the door. Once you're in, you see your selling skills to actually get you the job. Tom Jackson, in his book *The Perfect CV*, describes the ideal CV as a '. . . written communication that clearly demonstrates your ability to produce results in an area of concern to potential employers, in a way that motivates them to meet you'.

It's like sending out a mailing shot or placing an advertisement for a shop in the paper. You want to get the customer interested. The advertisement must concentrate on benefits to the customer. An advertisement placed in a newspaper crowded with similar advertisements has to attract attention, be easy to read, and be full of benefits to the reader. Otherwise the typical preoccupied reader will pass over it. If the advertisement is good, the reader will pay attention to it and probably decide to go to the shop to check it out.

Employers are like preoccupied newspaper readers. They are not reading every word; they are skimming through pages of similar CVs. So the easier it is for them to see a potential match between you and the job, the more likely they'll stop skimming and start reading when they come to yours.

The employer should be able to read your CV and determine just how your past experiences will benefit his future. This means you have to tailor your CV to fit the job.

You don't need a separate CV for each and every job you apply for. But you do need a CV that's relevant to the type of job you're pursuing – one that will emphasise your potential benefit to the employer and the company. Your CV should make it easy for the employer to relate your past experience to the position now available.

My daughter Laura now has three different CVs she uses when looking for work, updating each as necessary. They cover her three areas of interest: child abuse assessment and counselling; research and writing; and translating and interpreting. Laura has had experience in all of these areas, but to include everything on one CV would be foolish – if not impossible. But because she has the three CVs, Laura is prepared to follow any unexpected leads that may arise.

Word processors, of course, make it fairly easy to update or personalise your CV. If you don't have access to a word processor yourself, you can use a local service. Prices vary around the country, but most services will keep your information on file (usually for six months to a year), and going back to revise the original is relatively inexpensive.

CHOOSING YOUR SALES APPROACH: WHICH TYPE OF CV WILL SELL YOU BEST?

Like the direct mail letter, the CV is a marketing tool to get you in the door. Your CV should be designed so that it emphasises your strong points, and plays down your weaknesses. It must be benefit-oriented and value added and targeted to the specific job you're going after.

You've already done the preliminary work you need to create a good CV. Your CCI and AAAs will be your foundation. What you need to do now is put that information in CV form, in the style best suited to your own experience.

There are three basic types of CVs: the chronological, the functional, and the customised. You should choose the CV style that shows you in your best light, and the one you are most comfortable with. Whichever format you go with, remember to be result oriented. You aren't writing a CV to show off what you've done, you're trying to show employers how what you've done will benefit them.

THE CHRONOLOGICAL CV

The chronological CV is the most traditional type, used about 60% of the time. It is just what it sounds like: a chronological job history, starting with your most recent employment and working backwards. A chronological CV is best used to *emphasise job continuity* (either from one company to another, or steady advancement within one organisation). If your job history is pretty straightforward, and demonstrates growth and development, you'll probably want to use a chronological CV.

However, this is the CV that presents the most pitfalls, because we tend to think that listing our experience means just stating the company name and job title. But even when writing a straightforward chronological CV, you must remember the concepts of sales and marketing, and the difference between features and benefits. The features of your CV are those company names and job titles. But the benefits are what will get an employer's attention.

This is an excerpt from a typical chronological CV that doesn't list any benefit:

Work Experience

ABC SCHOOL SUPPLIES LTD (1982 – present)
Dept. Controller, Furniture Division
Responsibilities included coordinating four other department controllers, preparing monthly sales analysis reports, supervising staff of four.

WALTERS ELECTRONICS CORPORATION (1978–1982)
Assistant Dept. Controller
Helped conduct financial audits, wrote reports, put in a new computerised cost accounting system.
Sr. Account Receivable Clerk
Analysed accounts receivable systems, revised old system, improved collections system.
Education
B.A. Chelmsford College

An employer looking at this CV would learn where the applicant had worked, for how long, and what his main responsibilities were. But there's not much there to tempt an employer – there's no bait. Now look at the work experience the way I've re-written it:

Work Experience

ABC SCHOOL SUPPLIES LTD (1982–present)
Dept. Controller, Furniture Division
Reported to Chief Financial Officer. Coordinated four other department controllers in cost accounting and tax returns. Prepared monthly sales analysis and department comparison reports. Developed new cost accounting system *which resulted in £250,000*

tax saving. Supervised staff of four who *handled 30% increase in volume without adding additional staff.*

WALTERS ELECTRONICS CORPORATION (1978–1982)

Assistant Dept. Controller
Co-conducted financial audits. Developed reports and recommendations for M.D. and Chairman. Implemented computerised cost accounting system *which resulted in £80,000 annual payroll savings.*

Sr. Accounts Receivable Clerk
Analysed accounts receivable systems. Revamped system which *increased productivity by 25%.* Implemented improved collections system *resulting in collecting £26,000 past due accounts.*

WENTWORTH'S DEPARTMENT STORE (1975–1976)

Jr. Accounting Trainee
Trained in all accounting procedures, including posting and balancing, preparing reports and summaries, reconciling irregularities.

Education
B.A. Chelmsford College

Try this with your own work experience. Start with a simple chronological listing of all the jobs you've had.

Now re-write this list, concentrating on features and benefits. Look for the bottom line results that will get an employer anxious to meet you.

THE FUNCTIONAL CV

A functional CV highlights your accomplishments and abilities and puts your strongest selling points right up front. You should use a functional CV when: you're just entering the job market; you're re-entering the job market after a gap of any length; you're changing careers; you've had many different and possibly unrelated jobs; or if most of your work has been temporary, or freelance and consulting.

My daughter Laura put together this functional CV when she heard of a job opening as a counsellor in a crisis center. When she spoke to her potential employer on the phone, she found out that the job also entailed some research and translating skills. Just out of college, Laura's experience had mostly been volunteer work and college research. She decided that the best way to let the employer know that she had all the required skills was to emphasise them in a functional format. Here is Laura's CV:

Laura Weinstock
PO Box 456
Seattle, WA 98145
(206) 522-5485

Counselling

- Counselled sexual assault victims and their friends and family. Established better understanding for victims of their legal rights and what to expect in court.
- Coordinated work with attorneys representing battered women and children, decreasing duplicate paperwork, lost records, etc by 25%.
- Conducted Volunteer Recruitment and Training programmes. Increased volunteer staff by 40%.

Translating and Interpreting

- Translated materials on domestic violence and parenting for Spanish-speaking shelter residents, making information accessible to 50% more residents.
- Translated technical manuals for prestigious Colombian health organisation. Completed 2 weeks ahead of deadline.
- Interpreted for French and Spanish speaking clients of Bed 'n' Breakfast establishment, resulting in 35% increase in clientele.

Research

- Research and co-wrote report on U.S. sponsored Costa Rican Nutrition Project. Report was sent to Costa Rican Government.
- Researched and wrote article on the increase of malaria among NYC immigrants. Paper published in prominent medical journal.

Work Experience

1984–6   YWCA – Inner City Recreation Counsellor
1986–8   NEIGHBOURHOOD LEGAL RIGHTS CENTER – Volunteer

Education

B.A.   Cornell University

Laura wanted to emphasise her abilities in three different areas. The functional CV can also be used to highlight major accomplishments in a single field.

Try re-doing your chronological CV as a functional CV. First list your major accomplishments, whether in one or more field and then list your work experience.

THE CUSTOMISED CV

This is the most job-specific CV, and the one I recommend as the most effective sales tool. During your telephone interview with your prospective employer (which we'll discuss in Chapter 24), you find out as much as possible about the job. At least find out the job title, and some of the major responsibilities. Then you customise your CV so that your accomplishments and what is required match up as closely as possible.

This does take time but it's worth it; it makes it very easy for an employer to 'put you in his picture' – to see how you would fit into the job. The more specific and clearly focused you are toward the job objective, the fewer extraneous, and possibly negative, impressions you make.

This is also the most suitable CV to use if you don't have much work experience, or if you've changed careers several times, as it de-emphasises your work history. You may even want to leave out your work history altogether.

The general format to follow for this type of CV is:

1. Job objective, written specifically to suit this job.
2. Major areas of expertise, *emphasising transferable marketable skills*.
3. Examples of specific accomplishments.
4. Work history, if it is good enough.
5. Education, if it is relevant or outstanding.

Here is an example of a customised CV. Shirley McDonald is applying for a job as a Senior Sales Account Executive for a cable television company. Through her research, she discovered that the firm is a young, progressive organisation looking for 'real go-getters' who can expand their markets. Shirley included only those achievements and abilities that directly relate to this job opening. Her customised CV looks like this:

Shirley McDonald
21 Cedar Lane
Richmond
(071) 336-2256

Objective
Senior Sales Account Executive

Abilities
Dynamic, results-oriented account executive specialising in selling intangibles. Exceptional negotiating, problem-solving and closing skills. Proven ability to develop new markets and maintain profitable relationships with established clients.

Major Accomplishments

– Initiated new marketing concept which resulted in £1 million in new business over a two year period.

– Developed ongoing relationship with long-time competitor's client, bringing in £100,000 business.

– Ranked number 1 in sales team in financial year 1988.

– As manager, doubled sales productivity in 6 month period through revised recruitment and training systems.

Work History:

1986–present   UK Broadcast Media Ltd – Media Sales
1983–1986   Olympia Investments – Investment Sales
1982–1983   Midland Capital – Investment Sales

Imagine you're sending your CV to your Ideal Prospect for your dream job. How would you customise your CV in that situation; using the headings Shirley used in her customised CV.

CV DO'S AND DON'T'S

There are no hard and fast rules for writing CVs and many people combine the formats to come up with a CV that suits their needs and personal style. However there are some basic recommendations about what to do and what not to do.

1. Do have your CV professionally typed and reproduced on good quality paper. Your CV is the packaging that attracts the buyer. Make sure it says good things about you. Sloppy reproduction, typographical errors, and/or dirty, wrinkled paper will most likely mean your CV will go straight on the rejection pile.

2. Do keep your CV to just one page. Two is acceptable if necessary. If you go to three, it means you're not being selective enough.

3. Do use pound signs and percentages whenever possible, as in the direct mail letter. Include result-oriented information, not every single function you performed in each job.

4. Don't list personal activities. Do include business-related activities, associations, awards, abilities, etc.

5. *Don't list personal information*, such as height, weight, marital status, age, etc.

6. *Don't list references*. You don't want anyone who isn't strongly considering you to call your references. Give out references only after the employer shows real interest.

7. *Don't include salary history or the salary range you're looking for.* Leave that subject until the interview stage.

8. *Do have someone else check over your CV before you send it out.* Ask him to proofread it carefully and make sure there are no errors.

A CV ALONE IS NOT AN EFFECTIVE SALES TOOL

No matter which style of CV you choose, it's still not the most effective selling tool. A busy boss may quickly skim over your CV looking for what he thinks are his exact requirements. Never send a CV alone. Always include your direct mail piece as a covering letter to convince the employer to read the CV more carefully, and see how your experiences and abilities can benefit him and his company.

Some people send CVs with covering letters that read, 'As per your request, here is my CV.' This is nothing but a waste of paper. You want to use every selling tool you can, so send your direct mail letter along with your CV. That way, no matter which CV you send, the potential employer will still receive a personalised, benefit-oriented, targeted letter.

24

TELEMARKETING:
Tapping into Your Telephone Connection

'The only way to close a sale is to get to the real
decision maker'

PHONE PHOBIA:
ITS CAUSES AND CURES

I'll never forget my first job-hunting experience. I was ambitious. I was
enthusiastic. I was ready to go get 'em. I went over my CCI, reviewed my
accomplishments, researched my sources with great gusto, and sent out
targeted, well-written, benefit-laden direct mail letters. I kept an
appointment calendar next to my phone. If I wrote in a letter to Mr Joseph
Adams that I would call on the 13th, I would write Joseph Adams' name
in a bold, strong hand on the 13th. Soon I had many such names pencilled
in, and the day I sent my letters out I flipped through the calendar with
great anticipation. Everything was going fine.

Then it began to hit me. On the 9th I felt a slight twinge. On the 10th I
noticed I was getting a little jumpy, and by the 11th I was really starting to
sweat. As the time for making the calls got closer, my anxiety level
increased. I was afraid to pick up the phone.

What is it about the telephone that terrifies us so? I would think to
myself, 'What's the worst that can happen? Can the person on the other
end jump through the phone and harm me physically? Of course not. The
worst that can happen is that he'll say no.' But that 'no' loomed large in
front of me. One 'no' would send me scurrying back to do some more
research, write another letter or any other task that would keep me from
making the next call. I went through this with every call – until I realised
that my anxiety and imagination were getting the better of me, and my
fear of rejection was coming across on the phone.

'Phone phobia' is a common phenomenon. The fear of rejection is very strong; we take it all very personally. Not everyone you contact is going to buy. But all marketing campaigns are based on the law of averages: the more calls you make, the higher your average return and the more opportunities you have to practise your skills and build your confidence. Your job search is a marketing campaign; you have to expect that you will get a certain percentage of rejections. You may get 5 appointments for every 50 calls you make – but those 5 appointments will be with people who are truly interested in what you have to offer.

Phone phobia takes other forms as well. You may be embarrassed to call. You may assume that you're interrupting someone's busy schedule, using up their valuable time. The truth is that your time is valuable as well, and if you didn't have a good reason to call you wouldn't be doing it. You are calling with something of real value – an offer that can help solve the other person's problems, free up his time and benefit his organisation. If *you* don't believe in your value and the value of your offer, neither will he.

The phone is not your enemy, it's a natural extension of you. Before you begin your telemarketing campaign, practise making calls until you feel really comfortable using the phone. Call people not for business but for pleasure. Make more calls than you normally do. Now is the time to catch up on those calls you've been meaning to make for months. Call friends and relatives. Call stores for information, call the library for research information, call anyone you can think of so that using the phone becomes an easy, pleasurable experience.

Make sure you're physically comfortable as well. If you're calling from home, try to set a separate work area for yourself so you'll feel more professional. If you're calling from your present job, remove your phone from the clutter on your desk, so that it has a 'home of its own'. George Walther, one of the country's foremost experts on telephone communications, says in his book *Phone Power*, '. . . the physical space works as a "mental anchor". When you turn to that place in your [home or] office, you shift into your "professional communicator" mode.'

TAKE ADVANTAGE OF YOUR ADVANTAGES

You're all set up. You've got your phone areas designated, you have paper and pencil nearby, an appointment calendar, and copies of the letters you sent out. You're ready to make your phone calls. If your confidence is still a little shaky, remember that when you're making a call, you have several advantages over the person on the other end:

1. You know more about the person you're speaking to than she knows

about you. You know there's a strong possibility she'll be interested in speaking to you. You may know some of her problems, and are prepared to offer your assistance. She'll be impressed with your knowledge and preparation for the call.

2. The person on the other end is not prepared for you, while you have spent a long time preparing for this call. Since you are prepared, you'll be ready to handle any objections or answer any questions she might have.
3. You have a strong objective firmly in mind, which gives you the edge in the situation.
4. The person on the other end is being asked to make a quick and unexpected decision. The only decision you have to make is what to say next.

BREAKING THE PROTECTIVE SECRETARY BARRIER

One common problem you may face is that the person you wish to speak to is probably not the person who answers the phone. You want to speak directly to the decision maker; you want to speak to the person to whom your letter is directed. More than likely, you will first have to get past the protective secretary, who is answering the phone because the decision maker is in a meeting or is preoccupied.

Technique 1: Be Polite but Firm When you call and the secretary answers, immediately state who you wish to speak to. 'Ellen Paterson, please.' Don't ask a question, or even have a question in your voice. Make a statement as if you expect to be put through immediately. Many times you will be. But you should be prepared for a good secretary to do his or her job – and part of that job is to screen the boss's calls. However, secretaries are also used to fulfilling requests. Make yours one she can't resists. Repeat frequently that you want to be put through.

If he or she says, 'Please tell me what this is about?' or 'What is this in reference to?' you can say, 'She's expecting my call,' because she is (you wrote in your letter that you would call on this date). Or, you can simply reply, 'It's personal, please put me through.' This usually works right away.

The secretary's job is to screen out bothersome, unimportant calls. You shouldn't be calling if that's how you feel about the call you're making. You want to convey strength and conviction and the feeling that yours is a call worth putting through.

Technique 2: The Direct Approach You can try the direct approach by saying 'I recognise that you are protecting your boss's time. This will only take a minute or two. Please put me through.' You should try to build a relationship with the secretary, so that he or she will know who you are the next time you call; if you've built a good rapport she might put you straight through the next time. Always remember that the secretary is doing a job, don't argue or be offensive.

Remember also that the secretary can be a great source of information, starting with the boss's title and the correct pronunciation of the boss's name. This is an important point; people are very sensitive about their names. My son's name is Ian – pronounced Eye-an. All through school, he took an immediate dislike to any teacher who couldn't get his name straight. If you're calling someone with a difficult name, be sure to find out how to say it, then write it down phonetically on your copy of the letter.

And don't forget the secretary's name. Write that down also. If you call back again, be sure to use his or her name.

Since many secretaries have a good deal of influence with their bosses, you want them on your side. Many bosses won't even set up an appointment if the secretary says, 'That person was rude when she called.'

If the secretary has been helpful, don't forget to thank her. Tell her when you call. She'll remember that too.

Technique 3: Get the Message If the boss isn't available, ask the secretary when would be the best time to call back. Find out if the boss usually comes in early or stays late. Ask for a specific time to call back. If you say, 'When would be a good time for me to call again?' it implies that you're available to call at her convenience. You can say, 'I'll be available at two o'clock. Would that be a good time to reach her?' Let the secretary know that your time is valuable as well.

Don't be tempted to divulge your exact purpose to the secretary. There is an old sales slogan that goes, 'the more you tell, the less you sell' and that applies here as well. You don't want to give anyone the opportunity to rule you out or turn you away prematurely.

What if the boss is out when you call? Should you leave a message? Robert Shook, author of *Successful Telephone Selling in the 80s*, and *Telephone Selling Techniques that Really Work* says, '. . . you don't want to tell the secretary any more than is necessary, but if you keep calling back and don't leave a message, he or she will probably recognise your voice and become annoyed. You can leave a message saying "It's personal," or "It's confidential."'

Technique 4: Make the Telephone Operator Your Personal Secretary Another excellent way to get through to the decision maker is to use a person-to-person (or personal) call. This can be time-consuming and expensive, but it does work. You may not know it, but you can make local person to person calls. What you are actually doing is hiring the operator to serve as your secretary and make the call for you. You'll need a cooperative operator. If you don't get one, keep trying until you do.

After you dial Operator, ask him or her to hold the call because you have some instructions to give. Then say that you want to speak to Ellen Peterson – and only Ellen Peterson – and if she is not there to please leave a message that you called. That's all. When Ms. Peterson returns she will have a message that you called person-to-person. After two or three of these messages her curiosity will be aroused and she'll probably pick up the phone next time you call. One of the advantages to this is that people still have a certain respect for long distance (and especially person-to-person because so few people use it) – and if the operator says person-to-person they will assume it's long distance even if it isn't.

After three calls and three telephone messages from you, you can instruct the operator to inquire when would be the best time to call. You can then call back directly when you know the decision maker will be in.

The best time to call

From my own experience, I've always reached the people I've wanted to contact by using a combination of these phoning techniques. No person is unreachable if you really want to get through. The best times to connect with busy people are before work, during lunch and after work. If you have asked the secretary, you know which of these times would be the best to try. You might even try on Saturday mornings, when many executives come in to catch up on extra work and are without a protective secretary to take their calls.

WHAT TO DO WHEN YOU DO GET THROUGH

Finally, the secretary does put you through. Or isn't there. Or is out sick. You've made it past the bodyguard and now you're speaking to the decision maker. You must go directly after your objective. This is not the time to try and make small talk; you must grab attention immediately. One major disadvantage of the phone is that the other party can simply hang up on you if you haven't given sufficient reason for her to stay on the line.

You should always start off by using her full name. Say, 'Is this Ellen Peterson?' However, you may feel more comfortable saying Ms Peterson. Then follow immediately with your name, and the fact that you're following up on the letter you sent. This is important because you don't want her to spend your phone time thinking, 'Who is this person? Am I supposed to know him? What does he want?'

Once you've introduced yourself and reminded her of the letter, take a deep breath and go for it. Start right in with a powerful benefit, and then request an appointment.

'Ellen Peterson? This is David Clark. I'm the sales executive who wrote you a letter last week saying that I added 18 new accounts last year in a territory that was supposedly saturated with our product. I know I could do the same and more for your company. I can come in and see you on Wednesday the 10th at quarter to four, or Thursday the 11th at quarter to ten. Which would be best for you?'

The reason for the quarter hour is a subtle one. If you say you can come in at two o'clock or three o'clock or nine o'clock, the assumption is that the interview will take an hour, and she may not have an hour to spare. If you use the quarter hour, the assumption is that the interview will be only 15 minutes long.

Persistence pays off

Remember that your goal is to get an appointment. You must be persistent, because it's not very likely that the prospective employer will say yes right away. You will need to keep coming back to your objective.

Be prepared for all kinds of responses. You may hear, 'I'm sorry, I haven't seen your letter'. Your reply could be, 'I'm sorry you haven't seen it. But I would be very happy to tell you more about myself on Wednesday at quarter to four or Thursday at quarter to ten. Which would be better for you?'

Or she might say, 'I've seen the letter. That's all I need.' Then your reply would be, 'There is really much more that I could tell you in person. Would Wednesday or Thursday be better for you?'

If she says, 'Tell me more about what you've done,' give her one accomplishment that was not in your letter. Persist, adding, 'I can tell you more on Wednesday at quarter to four or Thursday at quarter to ten. Which is better for you?'

Keep coming back to your objective. If you tell too much over the phone, the employer may think she has enough information to make a decision right then. This is not what you want. If she says, 'I really don't have time to see you', say 'I know your time is very valuable, but also I know I have something valuable to offer. I will only take up 15 minutes of your time, and I'll be in your neighbourhood next week. Would Wednesday or Thursday be better for you?'

If she says she'll be out of town for three weeks, try and set up the appointment for when she returns. Offer to drive her to the airport, bring in her favorite breakfast – whatever it takes (within reason) to get that appointment.

You are using a technique called 'the broken record'. This technique involves calmly and persistently repeating your point. By remaining calm and pleasant throughout, you avoid being annoying, but you do get your point across. Be assertive, not aggressive. Be charmingly persistent. If the employer gets annoyed say, 'This same persistence, Ms Peterson, is an example of how I will apply myself to all my work.' Make it flattering to her that you care so much. Your objective will be reached when you get a definite response for an appointment.

Don't forget to network

Never hang up empty handed. If the answer is no, go for some leads. Ask if there is anyone else in the company (if it is large enough) or anyone she knows elsewhere who might benefit from your services.

Be specific when asking for referrals. This is a technique that I teach in my sales seminars. If you are selling coffee makers and you run into a no-sale situation, you might just say, 'Do you know anyone else who would like to buy a coffee maker?' Chances are the prospect will say no. But if you're more specific and say, 'Do you know anyone who's been complaining about the quality of their coffee lately?' you get the prospect thinking along a specific track. 'Oh yes,' he might say, 'My neighbour down the street was talking about that just the other day. She may be in the market for a good coffee maker. Let me give you her name.' The prospect is then doing someone else a good turn by helping to solve their problem.

So instead of asking, 'Do you know anyone else who might be interested in speaking with me?' ask, 'Do you know anyone who's been complaining that they can't find new markets in their territory? Perhaps they would be interested in seeing me.' You might get referred to a colleague in a related field who is a likely prospect. You can respond by saying, 'I appreciate that information, Ms Peterson. May I say that you gave me his name?' Then you can call and say, 'Ms Peterson of XYZ Company suggested I call you . . .'

YOUR ATTITUDE COMES THROUGH

As any successful telemarketer can tell you, your attitude comes across strongly and makes an immediate impression. If you're uncertain and apologetic over the phone, your prospective employer can only assume you'll be that way on the job. He or she is much more likely to respond to someone who sounds confident and enthusiastic.

Think about people you enjoy listening to, people you like. What are some of their attractive qualities? Are they optimistic or pessimistic? Do they express interest in you and the world around them or do they seem self-centred and preoccupied? Attractive qualities (qualities that are not only pleasant, but that actually *attract* other people) are not hard to acquire. Everyone has positive and negative qualities. But the more you focus on the positive qualities, the more dominant they become.

Natalie Tremain was out of work and depressed. Natalie (and many others at the plant) was laid off when the textile company she worked for was acquired by a large conglomerate. An excellent manager, Natalie knew many people in the textile industry, but she was losing momentum in her job search. She tried making calls, but after two or three unsuccessful attempts, she was reluctant to go on. She would stop and watch TV or do some errands. She would eventually make another call or two, then stop again. Finally, Natalie called her friend Joanne, another job seeker, to see how she was managing.

'Oh, I'm doing fine,' Joanne told her cheerfully. 'I've already got three interviews set up for next week, and I've got lots more calls to make.'

'Didn't you get a lot of rejections?' Natalie asked. 'How do you keep going?'

'Yes, I got some rejections,' Joanne replied, 'but I figured those people were losing out on a good thing and I went on to the next call. I schedule a time for making phone calls and then pretend that I'm at work and this is the job I have to do. I've spoken to some very nice people who seem really interested. I'm going to make some more calls right now as a matter of fact.'

Natalie thought about Joanne and her attitude towards rejection. She tried it out herself and found she was able to make several more calls that day. She even set up an interview with someone she's been particularly nervous about calling. When Natalie changed her attitude and her 'work' habits, the responses she got changed too.

If you admire what someone else is doing, imitate his or her attitude. Try it on for size. Associate with positive people. Natalie listened to Joanne and imitated her attitude. If someone you admire has a lot of enthusiasm for his work, follow his or her example and see what happens. Act as if enthusiasm is a part of you and soon enough it will be. Act as if you're interested in helping others meet their needs and soon enough you will be. You'll find that these truly are attractive qualities, and people will respond positively to them.

TRICKS OF THE TELEPHONE TRADE

Grab a person's interest through positive and negative motivation. Positive motivation persuades your potential boss that it is well worth his time to see you because of your specific offer:

'I added 18 new accounts to a saturated territory. I know I could do the same or more for your company.'

Negative motivation lets the boss know that there is something missing in his present way of working, and that you have the answer to this problem:

'I know that the south-east areas seems to be saturated with electrical suppliers. What you need is someone who knows how to find untapped buyers in this area – and having done just that for my last employer, I know I can do the same for you.'

Visualise. Try and imagine what the person on the other end of the phone looks like, so that you are speaking to a real person. Know what you expect from him. If you don't expect a positive response, why bother to call?

Be prepared before you begin. Have copies of your letters handy, and any phone numbers you will need. Have blank paper and pens or pencils ready. Keep your diary open next to the phone and make sure you have all appointments, personal and business, written down. You don't want to forget an important appointment because you didn't write it down, or make two appointments for the same time because you didn't have your diary handy.

See yourself on an equal footing with the person you're calling. You are just as intelligent, competent and deserving of success as the people you are speaking with. You have information and ideas that they need, and you are convinced that what you have to offer will benefit the prospective employer and his or her company.

Rehearse, relax and breathe deeply before you begin.

Use a technique called bunching. Prepare all your calls and know how many you will do at one sitting. Group them in geographical areas.

USE YOUR VOICE TO HELP GET YOUR FOOT IN THE DOOR

Your voice is your calling card. Since he can't see you, the person on the other end is going to judge you by how you sound. Your voice can be a great help to you, but it can also be a serious liability. It can give you away as being nervous or unsteady – or it can convey the impression of courage and self-confidence.

Pay attention to your voice if you want others to pay attention to you. Listen to yourself. Practise by reading aloud, reciting in the shower, reciting poetry in the car. Listen to how classically trained actors such as Peter O'Toole or Meryl Streep use their voices as instruments of feeling.

The voice, as we hear it over the phone line, is made up of several different components: speed or pace, volume, tone, and diction. Each of these can be worked on separately and then together.

Match the pace

Listen to how the other person speaks, and match your rate of speaking to his; a fast talker will have no patience with you if you are too slow, and people who speak slowly are usually suspicious of fast talkers.

If your speed is very different to his, he'll feel uncomfortable without knowing exactly why.

The average rate of speech is about 150 words per minute. People think at a rate four times faster than they speak, however. So if you are going too slowly, you'll lose the attention of your listener. Speak too quickly, and people won't be able to follow what you're saying. Pace yourself. Study public speaking techniques. Remember to breathe and take natural pauses.

You can practise pacing your speech with this rhyme. Say the first line very slowly, the second line quickly, the third slowly, and so on. Then repeat the rhyme, saying the first line quickly, the second line slowly, etc.

> *Hey diddle diddle*
> *The cat and the fiddle*
> *The cow jumped over the moon.*
> *The little dog laughed*
> *To see such fun*
> *And the dish ran away with the spoon.*

Not so loud

Many of us tend to speak too loudly on the phone. Speak in a normal tone, as if the other person were sitting right next to you. If they can't hear you, they'll let you know. Keep the mouthpiece about ½ inch (1 cm) from your mouth and speak in a calm, low pitch. Tape record your voice during a normal phone conversation and listen to make sure you speak at a moderate volume.

Practise controlling the volume of your voice by saying the word 'No' over and over again, starting very softly (almost whispering) and working your way to very loud (almost shouting). You'll gradually learn to recognise when you're speaking too softly and too loudly.

Variety is the spice of life

The telephone is not an accurate reproduction of your voice quality. People's voices sound higher over the phone than they do in person. Vary your pitch and rhythm so that you are not speaking in a monotone. Using a tape recorder helps because you need to make adjustments according to how the other person hears you, not based on how you think you sound.

To practice pitch and inflection, say the following, letting your voice follow the words:

> *Let your voice come down evenly, smoothly as a sigh.*
> *Then evenly up and ever so high.*
> *Hold your tones level and high today;*
> *then level and low tomorrow, I say.*
> *Let tone glide high,*
> *then slide down low.*
> *Learn to say no, no, NO.*

Or recite the 'do, re, mi' scale, going from a high tone to a low one. Or try counting aloud from one to eight, going up the scale and coming down again.

Your tone of voice reflects your attitude. Nervousness, resentment and unhappiness are all amplified over the phone. But so are sincerity and enthusiasm. Think about the image you are trying to protect. Keep a smile in your voice and a positive attitude and you will transmit these qualities across the wires.

Watch that diction

Sloppy speech makes a bad impression in person, but a worse one over the phone. Sloppy speech makes you appear less important, less valuable. If the person you're speaking to can't understand you, they'll soon lose interest in what you have to say.

Practise clear diction by enunciating the 'P', 'B', 'N', 'M', and 'W' sounds by saying 'PAPA', 'MAMA', 'NANA', 'BABA', and 'WAWA.' Make sure your lips hit each other and build your speed. Try longer phrases, increasing your speed as you go along: 'We have rubber baby buggy bumpers'; 'Peter Prangle picked prickly prangly pears'; 'Toy boat, toy boat'; 'She sells sea shells by the sea shore'.

Keep practising until you have an open throat, an active lower jaw, strong lip muscles and a flexible tongue that trips lightly over tongue twisters.

Details, details

Be sure your phone works properly. We've all had experiences of talking to people whose phones buzz and hum or blur the conversation with static noises. You don't want all your voice work to be spoiled by an irritating mechanical background noise. And never, never use speaker phones; they make you sound distant and uncaring.

Get comfortable before you begin. The better you feel about yourself and your set up, the more appointments you will make. Then you'll be ready for the next important step – the fact to face interview.

Don't stop now. The better you get, the more appointments you'll have. You're ready to move on to the next stage of your marketing campaign, when you'll use all the techniques you've been practising so far – face to face.

25

FACE TO FACE
A GUIDE TO THE ULTIMATE
SALE:
The Job Interview

'A sale is a series of planned questions to uncover needs,
build trust, answer objections, and gain commitment'

EXPLOIT YOUR NERVOUS ENERGY

You are a thoroughly prepared salesperson. You've studied your product
inside and out, you're confident of your abilities and qualifications,
you've done your homework on the company and person interviewing
you, you've practised and perfected your marketing skills. Now you're
about to put it all together face to face. A thousand questions must be
going through your mind. What do I do? What do I say? What should I
wear? What will he expect? What do I do if she asks me about salary?
What should I say about the fact that I never finished college? What if he
thinks I'm too old? What should I say about the time I got fired? Suppose
he says 'No'? Suppose she says 'Yes'?

Your heart starts beating rapidly; your 'fight or flight' response is
telling you to turn around and run; you're sure you've got the wrong day,
the wrong address, the wrong . . . everything.

Everyone is nervous before making a sales call. It's all right to feel this
way, it's a natural human reaction. Coping with interviews is not something that comes naturally. You learn how to. Don't let your nervousness
scare you away – use it to your advantage. Turn that surge of adrenalin
into positive energy; it will keep you alert and on your toes. Nervousness
becomes a problem when you aren't prepared for what you have to do – if
you haven't had enough information or practice.

You will find that your nervousness decreases in direct proportion to
the amount of time you spend preparing and practising your interview

skills. There's only one way to keep nervous energy from turning into debilitating fear – and that is to *be prepared*.

You're already better prepared for this interview than you think. You have a career inventory of at least 10 and probably more AAAs. You've spent sufficient time assessing yourself and recognising your value; you've done your homework and you have been steadily improving your ability to sell yourself. It's taken research, organisation, networking, initiative, confidence, marketing and selling skills, and perseverance to get you this far – and these are all skills any employer will value. You're well ahead of the game before you even step through the door.

Don't let your nervousness get the better of you. Don't fall into the trap of thinking that everything rides on this one interview. If you don't get this job, you will leave no worse than when you came in. And you will have gained valuable practice in handling interviews.

PRACTICE MAKES PERFECT

In any skill-building process there is no substitute for practice. Remember the first time you rode a bike, or played baseball, or sang in front of an audience? I'm sure you were nervous, and probably not very good. But the more you practised and repeated the experience, the easier it got and the better you got. The first time a pilot takes off in a 747 must be a nerve-racking experience. But after 20 or 30 flights it becomes second nature to the pilot. So it is with going for interviews. That's why you work to get as many interviews set up as possible.

Even before you go out on your first interview you can practise the interview situation. Have a friend or family member role-play with you. Use your research and background information to prepare a list of questions you think you might be asked (see Chapter 27). Have your partner play several different potential employers. Ask your partner for feedback on how well you listened, how well you responded and how you presented yourself in general.

During my job search, I went on over 60 interviews. I got so I couldn't wait to be interviewed. And I received several job offers – not because I was perfect for each job – but because I had honed my interviewing skills so sharply.

THE TWO-OBJECTIVE INTERVIEW

You have two objectives when you go for a job interview:

1. To get a job offer
2. To get information about the job and the company.

You always want to get a job offer. Even if you don't want the job, you want to secure a job offer: you can always turn it down. Not only is it good practice for you to go after the job offer, it's a confidence booster. Just remember not to lead people on and allow them to think you're going to accept a job if you have no intention of doing so. If you're called back for a second or third interview, and you've definitely decided this job is not for you, there's no point in wasting everyone's time.

The second objective is to find out as much information as you possibly can about the job, about the company, and about your potential boss. Without a lot of information from your prospective employer you'll never be able to make a sound decision as to whether or not you want the job – and whether to accept the job or not should always be *your* decision. Keep this in mind: you're not just going to be interviewed, you're also going to interview your prospective boss.

Every interview is a question and answer session, with both sides trying to get the information they need. An ideal interview situation should be give and take, with each person asking and answering questions.

HOW TO READ THE PROSPECTIVE EMPLOYER'S MIND

Through the entire interview, the employer is only asking you three things:

1. Do you have the ability to do the job – and can you do it better than the other people I've seen?
2. Do you really want to do this job – are you excited and motivated by it?
3. Will you fit in and be part of the team – and make me look good?

Therefore, each of your answers should be another way of saying I do have the ability to do this job well, I very much want to do this job, and/or I will have no problem fitting in with your team. Listen carefully to the question being asked. Which of these three categories does it fall under? A simple question like, 'When can you start work?' may be asked a) to get a factual answer, and b) to find out how excited or motivated you are to begin your new position.

Listen closely to all questions you're asked. The less you're thinking about yourself and what you're going to say next, the better the interview will go. If you're busy thinking instead of listening, you will lose your concentration. Suppose an employer is asking you a question about why you left your last job and you're busy wondering how much money he's willing to pay you. How will you be able to answer the question? It will probably take you by surprise and you won't be able to answer in a calm, intelligent manner.

Be responsive to the employer and he will be responsive to you. Be an active listener. Nod your head. Let him know you agree with what he's saying. Not only will you give better answers by paying close attention, but you will lose your self-consciousness and anxiety as you concentrate on asking and answering questions.

THE MORE YOU TELL . . .

Karen was being interviewed for a position as Assistant Convention Services Manager at a large hotel. The job required dealing with staff, suppliers and hotel guests. During the interview, the manager said, 'This job entails a great deal of problem solving. Can you give me an example of your problem solving abilities?'

Not having written out her AAAs beforehand, and not quite sure what the employer wanted to hear, Karen stumbled through a story of an argument she had with one of the suppliers at her previous job. Then, thinking perhaps this wasn't a good enough answer, she continued on and told two more stories of disagreements she'd had with her supervisor. Karen was a good worker and, told correctly, any one of these stories would have shown her to be a creative problem-solver. But because she wasn't prepared, and hadn't asked the manager exactly what he wanted to know, she came across as someone who couldn't get along with others. Once again, the old sales proverb holds true: The more you tell, the less you sell.

Answer *only* the question that's being asked. Answer truthfully, simply and directly. If you're not 100% sure of what the interviewer means, ask a clarifying question. Interviewers are notorious for asking questions that you should not or cannot answer properly without more information. Don't hesitate to ask for it. A favourite opening gambit by interviewers is 'tell me about yourself'. Interviewers will often ask this at the very beginning of the interview, before you've been able to get much information. You should always counter by saying, 'There's so much I can tell you, but I want to focus on what's important to you. What specifically do you want to know?'

The more general the question, the more important it is that you ask a clarifying question. If the interviewer says, 'What accomplishments have made you most proud?' You might say, 'I've done many things that have pleased me. What areas are you interested in?' Don't answer until you know what he or she values most. You can dig yourself into a hole if you're not careful; for example, they may be looking for someone who is highly detailed and quality-control oriented, and detail work may not be your strong point. A general rule of thumb is to *never answer any question unless you fully understand the reason behind it.*

SELLING YOUR BENEFITS

Don't forget the sales techniques you've been studying all along. You used the concepts of benefit selling in your direct mail letter, in writing your CV, and in securing an interview appointment. Remember your AAAs when you are answering the employer's questions. If an employer says 'This is a very busy office. I need someone who can keep track of many activities. Can you do that?', your answer might be, 'I'm very organised.' (That's a feature.) You could continue with, 'In my last job I created a wall chart that let everyone see at a glance the projects that were under way, who was working on each project, and when the due dates were. That way we were able to shift staff when necessary to meet a deadline. My department never missed a deadline in two years.' (That's a benefit.)

Never mention a feature without going on to mention a benefit. Study your AAAs so you can pull one out at any time and use it to sell yourself into the job.

Tough questions, selling answers

No matter how well prepared you are, tough questions will come up – questions that may make you feel uncomfortable or are difficult to answer. I've listed several standard tough questions below. You should anticipate these kinds of questions and be especially well prepared for them. The trick to handling tough questions is to answer in such a way that any possible negative is immediately replaced by a positive picture of yourself and your abilities.

For example, if you're applying for a job in a field in which you have no direct previous experience, the interviewer might ask, 'Have you ever worked in the garment industry before?' You might say, 'I've worked in interior design and I know a lot about fabrication and fabric designers.' Or you might say, 'In my last job I was transferred into a new division of the company, and my supervisors were very pleased with how quickly I learned and adapted my skills.'

Some other tough questions you might be asked:

'What are your major strengths and weaknesses?'
Always qualify this question by saying, 'What do you feel are the strengths necessary to excel in this job?' This is a great clarifying question, because it shows the employer you are someone who wants to excel.

You know what your strengths are from your CCI. Sell the Success Factors that relate specifically to this job and give examples of how you have applied those qualities. Reveal only your strengths, even if you disguise them as weaknesses. Everyone has weaknesses, but some are 'safer' than others. You might say that you tend to be a bulldog – you never let go of a problem until it's solved. Or you get impatient with people who don't work as hard as you do. Or you're too much of a perfectionist, but you're working on it. Occasionally, it's alright to admit to a minor weakness. For example if you're a super salesperson you might say, 'I closed three times as many sales as anyone else on our sales force. My boss would moan at me, though, because I didn't always do such a great job with the paperwork. But I have improved, and I'll continue to work on that problem.'

'I'm not sure that you have the experience (or training) to handle this job. Do you?'

This is a question you should be prepared for: you know from your research what this company is looking for. But the employer obviously sees something about you he likes, otherwise you wouldn't even be in this interview. He's looking to you to help him find a way to get around this problem so that he can employ you.

If you were selling vacuum cleaners, you'd know that your model is smaller than some others, and doesn't have as much sucking power. But yours can get into small nooks and crannies, places other vacuums can't reach. That's the benefit you'd sell. When you're selling yourself, look for the benefits you have that others (even those with more experience) may not possess. Be confident. Let the employer know how your other strengths and skills can more than make up for your seeming lack of experience.

You're in an interview for a position as executive assistant to the head of the fundraising department for a large medical centre. You haven't worked in fundraising before. You might say, 'It's true I haven't worked in a fundraising office before. But in college I was very active in the Office of Special Events. Even as far back as high school, I was involved in fund raising – I raised 75% of the money my choir needed for a trip to Washington, DC. I know your department puts on dinners and charity auctions, and I feel my background in college, plus my other organisational abilities, will be very helpful to this department. I'm ready to give 110% in order to make up for any lack of experience I may have.'

'How do you see yourself five years from now?'

What this question really means is, 'Are you going to be around for the long haul? Or do you just see this job as a stepping stone to your next career move?' Reassure the employer that you anticipate being very happy in the prospective job, and that you'll be looking for ways to continually improve and grow. Sell your sense of commitment, and give examples of your record of loyalty and reliability.

'Why did you leave your last job?'
You must never lie, or put your old job down. Another old sales proverb says, 'Never put down the competition. It just makes you look cheap.' Don't make excuses for yourself. If you were fired, say so (the interviewer will inevitably find out if you don't); you needn't go into detail, but give him a general reason why things didn't work out. 'My supervisor and I had very different ways of working and things just didn't work out. But I gave it a good try and learned a lot on the job while I was there.'

'What makes you think you're qualified to work for this company?'
A defensive answer would be to say, 'I've done . . .' and rattle off a list of reasons why you're qualified. A nondefensive answer would be to say, 'That's an interesting question. Actually, you're in a better position to answer that than I am. What do you feel is the one thing that would make me qualified?'

'Can you work under pressure?'
This is a definite candidate for a clarifying question. Ask the interviewer to explain what he or she means by pressure. You might find out this an extremely high pressure position, and not one you want to take. Or you may find out that you've worked under similar conditions before and would have no problem dealing with them on this job.

'Do you like working with people or things?'
This is a loaded question unless you know what the job is. You have to have more information before you answer it.

'What sort of money are you looking for?'
Never talk money until you know there's a job offer. No matter what, wait until the interviewer is sold on you. That might mean waiting until the second or third interview. *A good salesperson always establishes value before talking price.* First, you show the prospective buyer all the wonderful features and benefits of the product he's considering. Then, when he's convinced this is the one he must have – that's when you discuss price.

The more time the employer invests in you, the more he or she has at stake. If the employer asks you this question early in the interview, you can counter with 'Is this a job offer?' If that seems too direct, say 'I think it's more important that we talk about your needs first, and if I'm the right person for the job we can talk about salary later on.' Then ask another question: 'What would you say is the primary skill needed to succeed at this job?' Negotiating for money will be covered in Chapter 28.

YOU HAVE THE RIGHT
TO REMAIN SILENT

One of the great formulas of success came from Albert Einstein. He said, 'If A equals success, the formula is $A = X + Y + Z$. X is work. Y is play. Z is keeping your mouth shut.'

Remember that no law says you have to answer every question when it's asked. If a question makes you very uncomfortable, you can always try a diversionary tactic. You could say, 'Mr Smith, would you mind if I asked you a question that just came to mind?' And there are some questions that law mandates you do not have to answer at all. The Equal Opportunity Commission has strict rules about questions relating to age, criminal record, financial affairs, handicaps, marital or family status, race or colour, religion, or sex. If you feel that questions being asked in any one of these areas are not directly related to job requirements, you can legitimately refuse to answer (pleasantly, of course). For example, if working on Saturdays is a legitimate job requirement, a question such as 'Will you be able to work on Saturdays' is allowed. But it can't be used as a subtle (or not so subtle) way to find out your religious beliefs. If you have doubts, you may want to reconsider working for the person who asked the question.

ASKING QUESTIONS YOURSELF

In order to achieve your second objective – which is to get enough information for you to decide whether or not you want this job – you're going to have to ask questions.

You are following two tracks during your interview: The first and most obvious is 'What is your problem? What can I do to help?' The second is: 'Is this the right job for me?' Every question you ask should come from one of those two contexts.

Take control: don't be an interview couch potato

Dennis came to me because he had been looking for a job for almost a year, and hadn't had any luck. During my first meeting with him, I understood why. Dennis was a very passive personality (at least in an interview situation), and he seemed so laid back and unaggressive that it was difficult to see how he'd ever be successful.

We went over the rules of interviewing until Dennis became comfortable with taking a more active role in the process, answering questions with energy and enthusiasm and asking questions of his own. Within three weeks, Dennis had two appealing job offers.

Employers are looking for energetic people. They don't want you to sit through an interview like a bump on a log, letting the interview go by without having any input. Remember you're the salesperson here. You have to make the sale – it won't make itself. In order to do that, you have to take control.

You take control in an interview by asking questions.

What would you do with the rest of your life if you won a million pounds on the pools? I got you thinking about it, didn't I? Just by asking one question, I changed the direction of your thoughts. My book *Smart Questions For Successful Managers* is based on the fact that a question is one of the simplest, yet most effective ways of taking and remaining in control of any conversation.

By asking the right questions in an interview situation, you can steer the conversation in the direction you want it to go. The impulse to answer a question – any question – is automatic. A question is like an electric shock to the brain; we feel compelled to answer. This is true for you and for the employer as well.

The more questions you ask, the more control you have. Each time you answer an employer's questions, regain control of the situation by asking another question. For instance, if an employer asks you to describe your greatest strengths, follow your answer with, 'What would you most like for a new employee to bring to this job?'

If you sit back passively and let the interviewer pick you over to see if you are suitable, you won't learn anything about the job. You must be an active participant. Before the interview, make a list of questions you would like to have answered. Carry the list in your handbag, briefcase or pocket and don't be shy about pulling it out. Smart interviewers appreciate a flair for asking good questions and the thoughtfulness and professionalism it takes to prepare them ahead of time.

Choose your questions carefully. Always use open ended questions that require more than a yes or no answer. For instance, don't ask. 'Is this the kind of job where I would have authority to make decisions concerning budget?' Instead say, 'What kinds of decision-making authority would I have regarding budgets?'

Use some questions to get facts about the job itself. Use others to find out the employer's needs so that you can let him know how employing you would fill those needs.

THE RULES OF THE GAME

The interviewer usually sets the style and tone of the interview. If the interviewer is very good (and you can't count on this), he may suggest that you feel free to ask questions throughout the interview. A less secure interviewer may say, 'I'm going to tell you a few things about the job, and then ask you a series of questions. You may ask any questions you have at the end.' Usually they talk so much there is no time left for you to ask your questions. Alternatively he may not set up any game plan, leaving you wondering how he's going to proceed.

You have no way of knowing how the interview is going to be conducted until you get there. All the more reason for you to be thoroughly prepared. Do your research and you will already know enough about the company to be able to ask intelligent questions. So you are armed and ready.

When the potential employer sets up the rules, the next step is up to you. You may choose to go along with his game plan, or you may politely object. For instance, if he or she has stated that you should save all your questions for the end, you might interrupt at a point near the beginning and say, 'Excuse me, would you mind if I asked a question here? I need to clarify something you just said.' The interviewer probably won't realise that you are changing the plan, and will more than likely be glad to explain what he or she meant.

When you go in for your interview, assume it's going to be a normal situation with an even exchange of questions and answers. You want to get control immediately. Remember, the person who asks the questions gains control. Try to ask the first question – pleasantly and politely. You can begin by expressing interest in your interviewer or by making an observation about the office or view. If you've come through a recommendation, you might casually ask, 'How do you and Jaimie Gerard know each other?'

You will have keyed yourself up on the company before you applied for the interview. Make sure you are up to date on the latest company news by keeping an eye on the trade papers and financial pages of newspapers. Bring up what you know in conversation and ask questions about what you have read. In this way you will stand out from the competition.

Whether you ask your questions as the subject comes up (and you may have to bring it up), or read from your list at the end of the session, there are always questions you can ask to keep you in control and give you the information you need.

Most of your time should be spent asking questions and listening carefully to the answers, not talking endlessly about yourself without a sense of what the other person wants to hear. Your questions also give the employer clues about your interest level, and how well you prepared for the interview. You will be judged not only by the answers you give to the interviewer's questions, but also by the quality of the questions you ask.

One of the best interviews I ever had was with a very sharp and smart sales manager. Knowing I had had two previous careers, he asked what made me think I would be satisfied in this job since I had so many interests. I took my time and thought about it. Then I asked him, 'Does your job satisfy all your interests?' I was eventually offered the job, and I'm sure it was because of my reply to that question.

Some questions you might want to ask

- What are the key responsibilities of this job?
- What do you foresee as possible obstacles or problems I might have?
- In terms of my major responsibilities, how much actual authority do I have?
- What changes or improvements would you like to see in these responsibilities?
- Of the people who have had this job before, what were the characteristics of those who performed well? Of those who didn't?
- If you employ me, what would your specific expectations be?
- Why is the position open?
- What would you most like for a new employee to bring to this job?
- How many people have held this job in the last five years?
- Who would I be working with on this job? Is it possible for me to meet them?
- How is job performance evaluated here?
- How is it rewarded?
- Does the company promote from within? How, and how often?
- How many women and minorities are in middle to upper management?
- How are decisions made here?
- What is a typical day on the job like?
- What is your overall philosophy about training?

Questions for your future

Everyone wants a job with a future, and in these times of mergers and hostile takeovers, it's vital that you get information on where the organisation is heading. You don't want to give the impression that you are simply applying for this job as a stepping stone in your career. However, you do need to consider the future; the best time to ask questions regarding the company and its future plans is towards the end of the interview. Here are some suggestions.

- What are the career paths for new employees? For employees within the company?
- I see that the company is expanding its markets into eastern Europe. Where do you see the company moving?

- What are you doing in terms of human resource planning to make that happen?
- Have you had any major layoffs or cutbacks in the past few years? Do you anticipate any in the near future?
- If so, how would my job and/or department be affected?

The most important question you can ask for your future is:

- What can someone coming in at this level, and performing in an outstanding way, hope to achieve?

Make a list of at least 10 questions you would want to ask at your next job interview.

REMEMBER YOUR SELLING ABCs

When the interview is coming to an end, remember your ABCs: Always Be Closing. Don't be afraid to ask for the job. Say, 'I would like very much to work for your company. What can I do or say to help you make a favourable decision on my behalf?' The interviewer might just tell you what else is on her mind. You'll know what their objections are and how to deal with them.

If the interviewer says, 'I'll call you and let you know about the job,' don't be passive. Set a specific time for you to call him back. If you are refused and you really want the job, press for a second interview: 'Mr Smith, have you ever wished for a second chance to make a better impression? I'd like that chance, since I really want to work for you. Can we meet again next week?' This has worked for me in many cases.

GETTING IT ALL TOGETHER

Everything about the interview counts – from the minute you arrive to the minute you leave. Get there early if possible, and be polite and friendly to everyone you meet. Don't smoke or drink, even if offered. Coffee or tea is acceptable, as long as you make sure there is somewhere to put the cup and saucer down when you have finished with it, you don't want to be left holding it awkwardly throughout the interview.

Find out about the office environment before you visit. Is it formal or casual? Does everyone dress alike or do they prefer a creative flair? If you're not sure, conservative is always best. You can always wear something different to the second interview. I once went on a job interview looking too chic, wearing an avant garde coat, too much makeup (at least for this particular company), and a severe haircut. They were interested enough to ask me back and I had another chance. For my second interview I came back in a camel hair coat, just a touch of makeup and a different hair style. The boss said, 'You seem different.' Eventually I was offered the job (although I didn't take it), and I'm sure I wouldn't have received the offer if I hadn't changed my appearance.

The impression you make on the interviewer carries over into the job itself. If you position yourself as strong, capable and ambitious in your interview, you begin to establish your reputation and power base for the future.

FOLLOW-UP:
THE SECRET OF SALES SUCCESS

'I attribute a lot of my success in this business today to follow-up procedures I followed from the beginning of my career, Jackie Burton, president of Burton-Luch Public Relations, told me recently.

'When I first started out, I had to work very hard to 'sell' my clients to newspaper and magazine editors and TV producers. I made it a habit to follow-up my initial sales call with a personal note, along with any requested materials. I'd call again to make sure they had received the package, and perhaps give them another idea of how they could showcase my client. Every time I booked a client, my first order of business was to send a thank you note or card. I sent notes no matter how it turned out, because I knew the editor or producer spent time trying to make it work.

'These people remembered me, and later on, when I had other clients to promote, they were happy to hear from me again. Selling is a complex process, but for me, it's the follow-up that makes it work.'

Many top sales professionals feel the same way, and the follow-up should be an important part of your sales effort. The day after each interview you go on, the follow-up process begins.

Keep a record of how the interview went. You can make a form for yourself to keep on file. Here is a sample for you to copy or adapt:

Date of Interview: _____

Name of Company: _____

Address: _____

Name of Interviewer: _____

Title: _____

Phone Number: _____

Job Position/Title: _____

Main Responsibilities: _____

_____

AAAs discussed: _____
_____
_____
_____
_____

Salary or Range mentioned: _____
Follow-Up:
Thank you letter sent: _____ (attach copy)
To Call Back on: _____ Call Made: _____
Next Step: _____

Positive/Negative Impressions: _____
_____

Summary of Performance (What did I do well? What can use improvement? Was I well prepared? Did I ask enough questions?, etc.): _____
_____
_____
_____
_____
_____

No matter how you feel your interview went, follow up with a letter thanking the interviewer for the meeting. Include a brief reference to your most relevant AAA and remind him that you'll be calling at the time you discussed (and be sure you do).

One manager told me, 'I often judge job applicants by their follow-up actions. If a candidate is really interested in the job and is as conscientious as she says she is, she'll call me back. Then I know I can trust her word.'

THE EIGHT SECRETS OF A SUCCESSFUL JOB INTERVIEW

1. Be prepared.
2. Be ready to turn negatives to positives.
3. Ask questions to keep control.
4. Listen actively to the content and intent of questions you are asked.
5. Don't answer any question you don't fully understand.
6. Ask for the job.
7. Follow Up.
8. And practise so much that you will be relaxed and comfortable enough to let your best self shine through.

A good way to be prepared is to know the kinds of questions you'll probably be asked. Study the next chapter, practise with the questions provided, add some more of your own, and role play until you're ready to face any interview situation. You're on your way!

26

HOW TO HANDLE OBJECTIONS LIKE A PRO:
Answering Tough Questions

'The person who asks the questions controls the sale'

OBJECTION NOT REJECTION

Consider the following four tough questions posed by interviewers:

Interviewer 1: 'It doesn't look like you have much experience in this field. What makes you think you can handle the job?'

Interviewer 2: 'So you've been a volunteer for 5 years. Do you have any real work experience?'

Interviewer 3: 'You were dismissed from your last job. Why?'

Interviewer 4: 'You don't seem to stay at any job for very long. Why have you moved around so much?'

They are all questions you may have been dreading, but if you read them over you will find that not one of these interviewers said, 'I don't want to employ you.' What they did was ask a question or, in sales terms, raise an objection.

One of the hardest lessons salespeople must learn is that an objection is not equal to a rejection. As we discussed in Chapter 22 on becoming a salesperson, an objection is what you hear when a buyer hasn't yet made a positive decision.

Robert and Herbert Shook, in their book *The Complete Professional Salesman*, state that, '. . . it is very important for you, as a salesman, to realize that a "no" does not necessarily mean, "No, I definitely will not buy!" It means, rather, "I am not convinced yet; give me a reason *why* I should buy."'

When employers ask you tough questions, they're really hoping you'll show them the reasons they should 'buy' you for the job. If a prospective boss asks, 'Why were you fired from your last job?' and you answer, 'Personality conflict – my boss was uncommunicative,' what impression will you make? Perhaps your last boss couldn't communicate well, but that doesn't tell this employer why he should take a risk and employ you.

Instead of taking objections personally you must learn how to handle them and go for the close. The key to achieving this is knowledge.

Remember my motto, 'Success is Turning Knowledge Into Positive Action'? Well, this is the perfect place to make that motto work for you by using the knowledge you already have of yourself. In any interview situation, you have the home court advantage. You know everything there is to know about your 'product' – yourself, your background and your experience. That is your 'home court', and you take it with you wherever you go. Prospects have only limited information about you, and base their objections within those limits. They may come up with a few reasons to say 'no,' but there are hundreds more reasons to say 'yes'. You know that they are and they don't. Not yet anyway. Every time interviewers object, you have another opportunity to show them a 'yes' they haven't seen yet.

SIX SURE-FIRE STEPS TO HANDLING OBJECTIONS

When objections come up, you have the chance to answer the question, offer more evidence, restate your case and show the prospect the real value she is getting for her money. Here are six steps to follow to be sure each objection is handled to your – and your prospective employer's – satisfaction.

1. Be an active listener. Let the prospect know you hear, and understand, her concerns. Ask yourself, 'If I were in her place, wouldn't I have the same concerns?' Never argue or put the interviewer on the defensive. A simple statement such as 'That's a good point, I'm glad you brought it up,' or 'I understand how you feel', can let the prospect know you and she are on the same side. Don't interrupt or assume you know what the interviewer's going to say, even if you've been asked this question many times before.

2. Ask the prospect to explain the objection to you. Ask yourself, 'Do I fully understand the problem here?' If a prospect says, 'I think you may be overqualified for this job,' ask 'Why do you think so?' or 'What do you mean by that?' She might say, 'Well, I'm not sure we can afford to pay what you'll probably be asking.' Then you know she really is concerned with money, and not with your qualifications.

If you hadn't asked her to clarify her objection, you'd have wasted a lot of time trying to convince her you're right for the job. Once you know she's really objecting to the 'price', you can continue to establish value for her.

3. *Translate every objection into a question in your mind.* Treat each tough question as a challenge, not an obstacle. Ask yourself, 'What's the missing information that's keeping this prospect from going ahead with the sale?' When a prospect says, 'I don't think you have enough background in this field,' respond as if she had said, 'Can you tell me what other qualifications you have to make up for your lack of experience?'

4. *Answer the objection.* Ask yourself, 'How can I help this prospect solve his problem?' Everyone has the right to a question or an opinion, even it's wrong. Answer the objection by emphasising benefits. If a prospect objects to a flaw or weakness, don't try to ignore or gloss over it. Say something like, 'That's a very good point. It is true that I don't have a lot of experience in this field, but my background in social work is perfect for the kind of interpersonal skills and understanding you need for a job in human resources. And I'm very eager to learn.'

5. *Sell the benefits.* Ask yourself, 'Do I know which benefits are most important to this person?' The stronger the connection between your abilities and the prospect's needs, the fewer objections you'll hear. For example, you're being interviewed for a position as a bank customer services representative. You assume the boss is looking for an outgoing 'people person'. That's true, but she's also looking for someone who can work on his own, because she travels a lot. So you would do best in the interview by selling your independent nature.

6. *Confirm the answer.* Make sure that you've answered the objection with no misunderstandings. Ask yourself, 'Are we both satisfied that the issue is resolved?' Ask the prospect, 'Does that answer your question?', 'How do you feel about that?' or 'Does that take care of your concern?'

Practise these six steps before you go into a real interview situation. Call your favourite role-playing partners to come up with as many objections as they can possibly think of. Ask them to go from the sublime to the ridiculous, from 'You don't have the right qualifications for this job,' to 'My astrologer says the stars are not in the proper alignment.' Then the next time an interviewer starts talking astrology, you'll have your answer at hand and your technique well established.

MOST COMMONLY ASKED INTERVIEW QUESTIONS

Interviews make us nervous because we don't know exactly what we'll be asked. It's that old classroom syndrome: you know you know the material, you're pretty sure you'll pass the test, but you're afraid there'll be one question you just won't know how to answer. You break out in a cold sweat just thinking about it.

An interview is not a test. There are no right or wrong answers. As a matter of fact, the more questions you're asked in an interview situation, the better off you are, *because each question you're asked is another opportunity to sell yourself*. Every time a potential employer asks you a question, he or she is really saying, 'Tell me why I should employ you.'

Listed below are commonly asked interview questions. They are also excellent selling opportunities. Study the questions and think about how you would give a positive, benefit-oriented answer.

For instance, suppose an employer were to say, 'I see you only stayed in your last job for four months. Why didn't you stay longer?' How would you answer? If you weren't prepared, you might get defensive and say, 'It wasn't my fault. I had family problems and I had to go home and stay with my mother.'

A better answer would be, 'I was doing well on the job, but then my father had a stroke and I left to help my mother at home. I learned a lot during that time at home, and it helped me make a decision to go into this field . . .'

Use them for practice and role-playing. Ask a friend to study the list of questions and select those that are relevant to you. Then set up a mock interview situation. This is an excellent way to practise your selling skills, build your confidence, and get out from under the shadow of the giant question mark.

- Why are you looking for work at this time?
- Why do you think you're qualified to work for this company?
- Why did you leave your last job?
- What are the things you want most from a job: money, power, satisfaction, etc.?
- Name three people in your life who've influenced you most.
- Can you tell me about a problem you had in your current job and how you solved it?
- What do you do in your leisure time?
- What are the main responsibilities of your current job?
- What have been your major accomplishments in your current job?
- What impact did these accomplishments have on your organisation?
- What do you like most about your current job?
- What do you like least about your current job?

- What do you think are your greatest strengths?
- What do you think are your greatest weaknesses?
- What are your long-term career objectives?
- Why should we employ you?
- Why do you want to work for our company?
- Why do you want to change jobs (or careers)?
- Aren't you a little young for this position?
- Your work experience seems to be all volunteer. Have you ever had a 'real' job?
- How competitive are you?
- Are you willing to work overtime?

SELLING SPECIFICS: QUESTIONS FOR SELECTED JOB CATEGORIES

The questions above are asked in all kinds of interviews. You will also be asked questions that apply to the specific industry or position for which you are applying. Accountants, for example, may be asked questions that apply strictly to that field. You should develop several AAAs that pay particular attention to your technical and specialised skills. If you don't have direct experience in the field, develop AAAs that show how your own background and experience relate to those that are called for in this job.

Information interviews are good sources for finding out what questions you might be asked. Tell your information source that you're planning to look for work in her field, and ask her to give you an idea of the questions she might ask of a potential employee.

Take careful note of these questions; then you'll be prepared when they come up in real interview situations. Here are sample questions that might be asked in four of today's hot job markets. Read them even if your career choice is not one of the four; they are intended to show you the kinds of questions interviewers use. After studying them develop your own list of 5–10 questions you may be asked relating to your own field of interest. Use your research, your own experience and your information interviews to help you.

Accountant

- What different accounting activities were you responsible for?
- Did you develop systems and controls on your last job? Can you describe them to me?
- What computer systems do you know?
- What types of budgets have you worked on?
- What types of financial analysis have you done?

Computer Operator

- Tell me about the equipment with which you've had hands-on experience.
- Where did you get your training?
- What was the nature of the work you did?
- With what software are you familiar?
- Can you learn other systems easily?

Electronics Engineer

- Describe some unusual technical problems and how you solved them.
- Describe the different types of circuits you've worked with.
- Describe a project you worked on from conception to finished product.
- What management responsibilities have you had?

Employment personnel

- What kinds of jobs were you asked to fill?
- What were your sources for finding new employers?
- Have you ever written job descriptions?
- What job evaluation systems have you used?
- Were you responsible for any orientation or training programmes for new employees?

27

NEGOTIATING FOR YOUR FUTURE:

How to Ask for More and Get It

'A successful negotiation is a win/win situation – but the person who asks for more usually gets it'

I don't know about you, but I'm a die-hard movie fan, and I love to watch the Academy Awards. A few years ago, Sally Fields made a wonderful picture called *Places in the Heart* for which she won Best Actress honours. She was being recognised by her peers for an outstanding performance in her chosen career. She stepped up to the microphone and millions of TV viewers waited to hear her thank her mother, her father, her high school drama coach and her beautiful family for all their love and support.

Instead, she walked up to the mike, tears in her eyes, and said, 'You like me! You really like me!' It was a touchingly human moment – a reminder that no matter how rich or famous we may get, the ultimate achievement often appears to be having people *like* us.

Why do I bring this up in relation to negotiations? Because our ability to negotiate is heavily tied up with our self-image and self-confidence. Sometimes we are so thrilled just to be 'recognised' that we are willing to accept less than we deserve. If you have been searching for a job for a while and one is finally offered to you – especially one that you are very excited about – your first reaction may be to shout, 'They like me!' and feel lucky to accept what is initially offered.

The fact is that when you are offered a job, your bargaining power is greater than it will ever be. If you're saying, 'I'd better not ask for too much or they'll just employ someone else,' you'd better think again. You have just successfully convinced this interviewer of the valuable contribution you can make to his organisation. Don't undermine that effort by selling yourself short. The interviewer wants you for the job – and he doesn't want to begin the costly, time-consuming search process all over again. So you are actually in a very good bargaining position.

CHECK YOUR EGO AT THE DOOR

Negotiation is above all an exercise in logic and clear thinking. Whenever emotion supersedes your reasoning power, you have lost. If you let your ego get in the way and respond to a lower than expected offer with, 'Who do you think you're talking to! *I* can't accept an offer like that!' you're not going to get much further in the bargaining process. Getting angry or frustrated if things don't go your way doesn't help at all, it only gives the other person an advantage. Since negotiation is a form of problem solving, if you fail to communicate your specific problems, needs and bottom-line positions, you will probably not get what you want.

Negotiation requires objectivity. You may be tempted to take a job (a) simply because you like the person who is to be your boss, or (b) you think that he is such a nice guy he'll give you other concessions later. Liking your prospective employer is a consideration; however, that person may be fired tomorrow, or be transferred or promoted, or go to another company. Don't make negotiating decisions for emotional reasons.

CREATIVE PROBLEM SOLVING

Negotiation is nothing more than creative problem solving. We don't need to be mean or intimidating to be a successful negotiator. We don't need to manipulate or take advantage. The object of negotiation is to find a middle ground that is acceptable to both parties concerned. And it involves many of the skills we have previously discussed, especially evaluation, decision making and communications.

Communication is the key to negotiation. The better you can communicate what you want and why you want it, the better your chances of getting it. We're back to the principles of good salesmanship again – if you can demonstrate the benefits of your suggestions to the other person, he's likely to agree with you.

THINK POSITIVELY

As Herb Cohen, negotiating expert and author of *You Can Negotiate Anything* points out: 'Power is based upon perception – if you think you've got it then you've got it. If you think you don't have it, even if you've got it, then you don't have it.' If you seem convinced that what you are asking for is fair and proper, then others will be convinced too.

Anyone can be a good negotiator. Many of us are afraid to ask for what we want because we don't feel we deserve it. When you are negotiating, it doesn't matter how you feel. It's how you *act* that counts. Think of what is more important to you: living through a feeling of uncertainty and discomfort for a short while, or living for a long time with the consequences of being unable to stand up for yourself. Feelings pass quickly. You may never get another chance at this negotiation again.

Ted and Frank were both job hunting at the same time. Each was offered a job as a purchasing agent at a large manufacturing firm. Ted was offered a starting salary of £14,000. He had hoped for at least £15,000, but was afraid he would blow the deal if he asked for anything more. He accepted the offer.

Frank was also offered £14,000 to start. He, too, was willing to accept the money – providing he was assured a place in the company's training programme, and tuition reimbursement towards his M.B.A. The employer agreed.

Five years later, Ted was struggling to pay for night school in order to earn his degree. Though he had moved up to a supervisory position, without further training he had very little opportunity of moving up further. Frank, on the other hand, completed his M.B.A. and did so well in the company training programme, that he was promoted to a management position after only three years. There was very little difference between Ted and Frank in terms of ambition or ability. The major difference was in their attitude towards negotiation at the time they were recruited.

THE ULTIMATE SALES GOAL:
MUTUAL SATISFACTION

Negotiating is something we all do frequently in our daily lives without even being aware of it. We negotiate for who will take out the rubbish, or who will drive the kids to school. We negotiate about which video to hire, or whether to have a Chinese take away or go out to a burger restaurant. We give a little, we get a little.

Negotiating is a specialised form of problem solving. There are some problems that you can solve yourself. Problem solving becomes negotiation when two people or groups start from opposing positions and attempt to find a compromise, each side hoping to give up as little as possible, and to gain without the other side losing.

Every business owner knows a deal isn't clinched until all the details are ironed out, the price settled and the goods delivered. All the selling skills you've been learning and practising throughout the job search culminate in negotiating the price of your product.

Negotiating is not about winning. It's not about making unreasonable demands and expecting others to 'take it or leave it'. Negotiating is about options. It's about asking yourself and your opponent one important question: 'How can we come to a mutually satisfying agreement?'

You do this by posing 'What if . . . ?' situations. 'What if I give you this and you give me that? Would that satisfy both our needs? What if I take less of this and more of that? Would that be agreeable?' The more options you come up with, the more room you have to compromise.

KNOW WHAT YOU WANT

If you don't know what you want out of a job you'll be tempted to take anything that's offered without examining the consequences. There are many other factors to consider besides money. You must clearly decide what is most important to you.

A young friend of my daughter's came to me for advice about a job she'd been offered as an editorial assistant on a small magazine. It was a publication Linda admired and respected, and she was thrilled to be offered a position there. But they couldn't afford to pay as much as Linda would have liked. She was prepared to go into negotiations and fight for a much higher salary.

We sat down and went over her goals. Making a lot of money was not as important to Linda as was having a career in journalism. This magazine would be fertile ground for a young journalist's 'on-the-job' training. When she thought about it, Linda realised she was willing to accept less money if they were willing to give her a chance to write.

In negotiations, it came out that the magazine was agreeable to giving her occasional short assignments with the possibility of full length articles later on. She took the job. Linda later told me that even if she had been able to get that higher salary, she wouldn't have been happy there without the writing opportunities.

Before our discussion, Linda was prepared to go in and battle for more money. But that wasn't what she needed to make her happy. *Had she not clarified her goals, she might have blown the whole deal for something that was not her highest priority.*

KNOW YOUR LIMITS

The next step after clarifying your goals is to set your limits. Start with what is least acceptable. Linda was able to accept a lower salary than she had hoped for, but she wouldn't have been able to work for no money at all. She had her rent to pay. Before she went into negotiation, she had to determine what was the lowest figure she could realistically accept. You have to know your cutoff point and resolve that you can't accept anything below it.

Next, determine the maximum you can ask for within reason. If you're negotiating for a company car, you can't reasonably insist that it be a Rolls Royce. Start with the maximum reasonable request and hope that you'll get it. If you don't, you negotiate down from that point. You never want to let your opponent know what your least acceptable level is or he'll go right for that. If you ask for too much you can always settle for less, but if you ask for too little, it's almost impossible to bargain upwards.

In order to help you set your goals and determine your range of acceptable compromise, answer the following questions:

- What do you want to get out of this job?
- What are your real needs (other than money)?
- What is the most you could get?
- What is your bottom line?
- Where specifically can you compromise?
- What concessions could you make that would hurt but are possible?
- Do you have a clear understanding of what's at stake, what issues are involved, and all your bottom-line limitations?

ADAPTING THE PERFECT PLAN

Don't be upset if things don't go exactly as you planned. A good negotiator is always flexible. Patience is valuable in negotiations, but you may also need to be quick – to alter your strategy, to pick up on a new factor or to go in a different direction altogether. Trust your instincts and allow yourself to absorb new facts as they are presented. Remember that one of the most sought-after Success Factors is Adaptability. Your demonstration of this factor can convince the employer he's made the right choice – and he may be more willing to see things your way.

As you are presented with shifting opportunities, you may decide to forego certain prizes in order to get new ones. Stay alert to these shifts by constantly asking yourself these questions throughout the negotiations:

- Why is the employer insisting on this particular point?
- How does this affect my bottom line?
- Am I still within my range?
- If the employer makes this particular concession, how can I help him save face?

MONEY TALK

Never talk money until you know there's a job offer. By the time you're talking money, the interviewer should be really sold on you. The more time he or she has already invested in you, the more you're worth.

There is a principle of economics that is particularly applicable here, and that is, 'Money follows value.' If you (or the employer) want to talk about money before you've established your value, you'll be on the short end of the stick.

In most cases, you don't want to discuss money until the second or third interview. At that point, you'll have a pretty good idea of the employer's level of interest. You will also have gathered enough information about what the job entails to make an evaluation of how much you think you should be paid. If an employer asks very early on, 'How much money are you looking for?', he may be trying to screen out candidates. He may really be asking, 'Are you over-qualified for this position? Or under-qualified?'

You should answer this question early in an interview. You can easily and calmly reply, 'It's too early to discuss salary at this point. I don't know enough about you or how I can help you and your company. Then you can change the subject by asking a question – because the person who asks the questions gains control of the conversation. Should the employer then return to the subject of salary, go for a trial close. 'Does this mean I have the job?' or 'Is this an offer?' If he says no, then repeat the fact that it's too early to discuss money, and ask another question.

GETTING DOWN TO BRASS TACKS

When you do reach the point when 'money talk' is appropriate, try to get the employer to mention the money figure first. If you get him to disclose his acceptable price range you will then know whether or not it's even worth pursuing the job. You may find it's even better than you hoped, and if you had suggested a figure first, it would have been too low.

When the interviewer asks you how much money you're looking for, you should ask whether there's a possibility of negotiating. Some salaries are fixed – the employer doesn't have any power to negotiate. Many jobs have a salary range that can be discussed. Some jobs have an unlimited salary budget. So ask the employer directly which category this job fits into. If you're asked 'What are you looking for?' say (with a sense of humour), 'What I think I'm worth and what you think I'm worth may be very different. What are you offering?'

If the job has a salary range, ask what the range is. If the employer says,

'The range is £12,000 to £14,000' you should reply, '£14,000 sounds like an acceptable figure.'

If the employer asks 'What's the minimum salary you would accept?', don't answer. Tell her you're not looking for the minimum. Say, politely, that you are looking for a job that is both intellectually (or creatively, or whatever is important to you) challenging as well as financially rewarding.

One important piece of advice is never to accept an offer immediately, even if you think it's a good one. Let the employer know that you're seriously interested, and that you know you could make an outstanding contribution to this company, but add that you need to consider the offer for a few days. The employer will wonder what other offers you're considering, and may even increase the offer in a few days' time. If not, you can always call and say you've decided to accept the offer.

Thinking it over also gives you the chance to make sure you have negotiated well and got what you needed. Once you've made an agreement, you can't very well go back and say, 'By the way, I forgot to ask for . . .' If you've asked for time to consider the offer, you can say, 'I've been thinking over your offer and on the whole it seems very fair. But we haven't discussed . . .' That way, you still have the negotiations within your control.

PLAYING YOUR CARDS RIGHT

Negotiating, like poker, is not always about holding the best cards. A good poker player is always looking around, staying aware of body language and non-verbal signals – yours and the other player's. Your eyes can reveal a lot about you. When you're asking for what you want, look directly at the other person. If you're constantly shifting your gaze or looking down, the implication is that you don't believe in what you're saying. You have nothing to be embarrassed about. It's okay to ask for what you deserve.

Never treat your counterpart lightly. Listen attentively and agree as much as possible that his suggestions are good, although perhaps not what you had in mind. If you disagree, do so respectfully. The best way to turn a negotiator hostile is to make him feel his suggestions are being dismissed or ignored.

Pay attention to how the other person is acting. Ask yourself, 'Is this person sending any non-verbal signals? If so, what do they mean?' Such signals can tell you when to hold the line and when to push forward. If you're in an interview and the prospective boss is giving you her full attention, then suddenly begins to fidget in her chair, perhaps you've said something to turn her off. Try and find out what it was, or ask a quick question to change the subject.

THERE'S MORE AT STAKE THAN MONEY

We negotiate in order to meet our needs. Companies, in the past, have assumed that all its workers' needs were the same, and benefits were designed for the average worker. It wasn't practical to make a separate deal for each person – the book-keeping and paperwork would have been too complicated.

Today much more emphasis is paid to individual needs. Computerised systems make it possible for even large organisations to devise customised benefits plans. It's up to the individual to make sure she has the ability to negotiate for those things she deems most important.

Before you begin your negotiations for your new job, sit down and make a list of all the possible factors that would make this the ideal job for you. Here are some of them:

- *Monetary:* salary, salary potential, bonuses, commissions, profit sharing, royalties or residuals.
- *Position:* title, authority, responsibility, office, support staff, budget, career potential.
- *Benefits:* life and health insurance, pension scheme training, holiday entitlement, flexible working hours, child care facilities or allowance, tuition reimbursement, company car.

THE 15 SECRETS TO NEGOTIATING POWER

Getting what you want takes a winning combination: asking the right questions, mastering your selling skills, and a strong belief in your worth and value to the job. It also takes practice in skilful negotiating tactics. Here is a summary of what it takes to be an effective negotiator:

1. In order to plan your negotiations, you have to have a good idea of the potential employer's wants and needs.
2. You are in your strongest negotiating position when you are first offered the job.
3. Before you begin negotiations you should conduct a careful economic analysis of what you would like to get from the negotiations, what you would be willing to settle for, and what is your bottom line.
4. You should show a sincere personal interest in the employer as well as interest in the company, and talk in terms of those interests.
5. Negotiating with a win-win attitude will generally result in a more equitable result than a competitive 'me-against-you' attitude.
6. It is usually a good idea to take up less controversial issues first, and establish areas of agreement and an attitude of acceptance.

7. You must always establish value before you begin negotiations.
8. Your eyes give you away. Look directly at your negotiating partner without wavering or lowering your lids.
9. The mouth is also a give-away. Always begin negotiations with a warm smile, even if you think you're about to disagree.
10. You come to an agreement only when a final concession is made by one person who feels that the other party will make no further concessions.
11. One of the best and most effective ways to have your negotiating partner accept your position is to have him participate in the reasoning process that leads to your point of view.
12. Always be an active, attentive listener. You may not agree with the other position, but you should never ignore it.
13. Before you leave the negotiations, always sum up the key points so you are sure that both parties have a clear understanding of the agreement.
14. Be honest and fair, and expect your counterpart to be the same.
15. Studies show that a negotiator who initially asks for more and offers to give up less usually winds up obtaining more and giving up less.

By this point you have become a super salesperson. Don't sell yourself short. You know the value of your 'product', and your value to the employer. You're not asking for anything you don't deserve. You're not trying to get something for nothing. Negotiating is a way for both of you to come out ahead. Keep this in mind, and you'll always be a winner. It's your work, it's your life. It's your choice. Don't settle for less than you want, or less than you deserve.

28

A FINAL LOOK FORWARD

'Marketing yourself is a lifelong process; use it well and
enjoy your success'

MARKETING YOURSELF CONTINUES . . .

Ask a millionaire how he (or she) has done what he's done, and he'll most
likely tell you, 'blood, sweat and tears'. Ask a millionaire *why* he's done
what he's done, and he'll probably tell you, 'for the love of it'.

One reason I wrote this book was to get an important message across:
the real secret to success is to love the work you do. On average we spend
96,000 hours of our life working – how sad to spend all that time unhappy,
underpaid and unfulfilled.

Marketing Yourself has given you the tools for success. You've learned
how to be sold on yourself, and how to sell yourself without selling out.
You've discovered what qualities employers consider essential in the
people they recruit, and how to improve and enhance your own Success
Factors. You've explored your options and then created a marketing plan
that gives you focus and direction. I've shown you how to use professional
sales techniques to get employers to buy what you're selling. The rest is
up to you. *Success is turning knowledge into positive action.*

TAKE A RISK: GET THE REWARD

The sales and marketing skills you've learned here give you choices about
your work you never had before – and make it possible to combine the
work you love to do with the thousands of options that are out there now
and are growing every day.

I know that it's not always easy to follow your dreams. There are bound to be problems and setbacks. But I believe in the power of setting goals and working towards them.

Who knows what the future will bring? World events are more astonishing every day. At the end of the 19th century, no one could have foreseen how rapidly the world would change. The 21st century will bring political and technological changes no one now can foresee or imagine. What I do know about the next hundred years is that we will have to make many choices in our lifetimes. It will be the Century of Choice and Change.

The basic principles and sales techniques presented here will enable you to market your talents and abilities into the 21st century. The more you welcome the future's visions of challenge and possibility, the more you'll get in return.

If you are resistant to change, you may see the future as a time of chaos that will disrupt your life.

But if you embrace change, you'll do very well in the years ahead.

Perhaps we should take a hint from the Chinese language: the symbol for 'crisis' in Chinese is made up of two parts – one for risk and one for opportunity. You can't have one without the other, and you don't get the reward without the risk.

YOUR MARKETING FOUNDATION: THE 30 BASIC PRINCIPLES

The future is yours for the taking. Marketing yourself is a process fuelled by your dreams and accomplished by solid sales and marketing techniques. The 30 basic principles behind this process are the foundation for a lifetime of career planning success:

1. Marketing success depends on the quality of the product and the ability of the salesperson.
2. Attitude is more important that aptitude for sales and marketing success.
3. If you don't believe in the value of your product, no one else will either.
4. An effective marketer isn't resistant to change, but views it as a challenge and an opportunity.
5. With so many similar products and services today competing for the same markets, the commitment of the salesperson is often the deciding factor.
6. Increase your selling power by improving your communications: be sure that your message is received the way you intended it to be.

7. Selling is creative problem solving: how best to get what you want while giving the customer what he or she needs.
8. Marketing often requires quick and confident decisions. That doesn't mean you have to be right all the time – we learn from all our choices.
9. The best sales question you can ask yourself is, 'How can I do it better next time?'
10. Marketing must be consistently future oriented for a product or service to survive in a rapidly changing world.
11. The more we rely on our own sales and marketing abilities, the more self-assured we become.
12. Interdependence and trust are the essential relationship builders.
13. The success of Value Added Marketing lies in knowing what people want and giving them more than they expect.
14. The more you know about your product, the easier it is to sell.
15. Success comes from building on your strengths, not from correcting your weaknesses.
16. People want to know the features, but they buy for the benefits.
17. You sell a product best by selectively emphasising features and customising benefits.
18. Effective marketing is the result of careful planning.
19. A successful marketing plan is based on understanding current economic trends.
20. You increase the odds of making a sale by knowing what the buying public wants and needs.
21. The odds continue to increase by knowing specifically where your buyers are located.
22. The art of closing a sale is the ability to sell to the right person in the right way at the right time.
23. The secret desire of every prospective buyer is, 'Make me an offer I can't refuse!'
24. In the age of customer service, mass marketing is not as effective as an individually customised sales approach.
25. Packaging has a major impact on why a customer purchases a product or service.
26. The only way to close a sale is to get to the real decision maker.
27. A sales is a series of planned questions to uncover needs, build trust, answer objections and gain commitment.
28. The person who asks the questions controls the sale.
29. A successful negotiation is a win/win situation – but the person who asks for more usually gets it.
30. Marketing yourself is a lifelong process; use it well and enjoy your success.

THE VALUE OF DREAMS

Never underestimate the value of your dreams. Your future success is based on the dreams you have today. Ignore the scenes of the past that told you otherwise.

Eleanor Roosevelt once said, 'The future belongs to those who believe in the beauty of their dreams.' Those who truly believe in their dreams are willing to work for them, to take the necessary steps to turn fantasy into reality, and wishful thinking into positive action.

Jack Lemmon, one of my favourite actors, is an example of someone who followed his dreams. His father, a baker, envisioned the day when he would proudly bring his son into the family business. When Jack announced he was going to New York to become an actor, his father was heartbroken.

His father asked, 'Is this your dream, Jack?'

Jack said yes.

'Do you love what you do, Jack?' his father asked.

Jack said yes again.

'Then go and do it,' his father said. 'I understand what it means to love your work. The day that I don't find romance in a loaf of bread is the day I quit.'

I couldn't agree with him more.

BIBLIOGRAPHY

Abrams, Kathleen S. *Job Prep 2000*. Wassau, WI: Entwood Publishing, Inc., 1986.

Avis, Warren. *Take a Chance to be First*. London: Macmillan, 1990.

Beatley, Richard H. *The Five-Minute Interview*. New York: John Wiley & Sons, 1986.

Beck, Joel. *Telephone Prospecting and Marketing*. Phoenix, AZ: General Cassette Corp.

Bettger, Frank. *How I Raised Myself From Failure to Success in Selling*. New York: Prentice-Hall, 1949.

Bolles, Richard Nelson. *What Color Is Your Parachute?* Berkeley, CA: Ten Speed Press, 1987.

Boyan, Lee. *Successful Cold Call Selling*. New York: AMACOM, 1983.

Butler, Diane. *Futurework: Where to Find Tomorrow's High-Tech Jobs Today*. New York: Holt, Rinehart & Winston, 1984.

Cetron, Marvin and Marcia Appel. *Jobs of the Future: The 500 Best Jobs – Where They'll Be and How to Get Them*. New York: McGraw-Hill Book Co., 1984.

Cohen, Herb. *You Can Negotiate Anything*. Secaucus, NJ: Lyle Stuart Inc., 1980.

Cornish, Edward, ed. *Careers Tomorrow – The Outlook for Work in a Changing World*. Bethesda, MD: World Future Society, 1983.

Danna, Jo, Ph.D. *Winning the Job Interview Game*. Briarwood, NY: Palomino Press, 1985.

Didsbury, Howard F., ed. *The World of Work: Careers and the Future*. Bethesda, MD: World Future Society, 1983.

Elam, Houston G. *Marketing for the Non-Marketing Executive*. New York: AMACOM, 1978.

Feingold, Norman S., and Norma Reno Miller. *Emerging Careers: New Occupations for The Year 2000 and Beyond*. Garrett Park, MD: Garrett Park Press, 1983.

Feingold, Norman S., and Avis Nicholson. *Getting Ahead: a Woman's Guide to Career Success*. Washington, DC: Acropolis Books, 1983.

Fraser, Jill Andresky. *The Best U.S. Cities for Working Women*. New York: New American Library, 1986.

Garfield, Charles. *Peak Performers: The New Heroes of American Business*. New York: Avon Books, 1986.

Girard, Joe. *How to Sell Yourself*. New York: Warner Books, 1979.

Girard, Joe with Robert Shook. *How to Close Every Sale*. London: Piatkus, 1990.

Gondolfo, Joe with Robert Shook. *How to Make Big Money Selling*. New York: Harper & Row, 1984.

Half, Robert. *Robert Half on Hiring*. New York: Plume Books, 1985.

Half, Robert. *The Robert Half Way To Get Hired in Today's Job Market*. New York: Bantam Books, 1981.

Hill, Napolean. *Think and Grow Rich*. New York: Fawcett Crest, 1960.

HMSO *Employment for the 1990s*. London, 1988.

Hopkins, Tom. *How to Master the Art of Selling*. New York: Warner Books, 1982.

Irish, Richard K. *Go Hire Yourself An Employer*. Garden City, NY: Anchor Books, 1973.

Johnston, William B., and Arnold H. Packer. *Workforce 2000: Work and Workers for the 21st Century*. Indianapolis, IN: Hudson Institute, 1987.

Krannick, Ronald L., Ph.D. *Re-Careering in Turbulent Times: Skills and Strategies for Success in Today's Job Market*. Manassas, VA: Impact Publications, 1983.

Lathrop, Richard. *Who's Hiring Who*. Berkely, CA: Ten Speed Press, 1977.

Leeds, Dorothy. *Smart Questions For Successful Managers: A New Technique for Effective Communication*. London: Piatkus, 1989.

Leeds, Dorothy. *PowerSpeak: The Complete Guide to Public Speaking and Presenting*. London: Piatkus, 1988.

Levinson, Jay Conrad. *Guerrilla Marketing: Secrets for Making Big Profits from Your Small Business*. New York: Houghton Mifflin Co., 1984.

Lewis, Herschell Gordon. *Direct Mail Copy That Sells*. Englewood Cliffs, NJ: Prentice-Hall Inc., 1984.

Ling, Mona. *How to Increase Sales and Put Yourself Across by Telephone*. London: Prentice-Hall, 1980.

Lund, Philip R. *Compelling Selling*. London: Papermac, 1988.

Maltz, Maxwell, M.D. *Psycho-Cybernetics*. New York: Pocket Books, 1960.

Marshall, Austin. *How to Get A Better Job*. New York: Hawthorn Books, Inc., 1964.

Naisbitt, John. *Megatrends*. London: Macdonald, 1984.

Nash, Edward. *Direct Marketing Handbook*. Maidenhead: McGraw-Hill, 1984.

Nierenberg, Gerard I. *The Art of Negotiating*. New York: Cornerstone Library, 1968.

Pascarella, Perry. *The New Achievers*. New York: The Free Press, 1984.

Payne, Richard A. *How to Get A Better Job Quicker*. New York: Signet Books, 1972.

Pell, Arthur R., Ph.D. *How to Sell Yourself on an Interview*. New York: Prentice Hall Press, 1982.

The Prentice-Hall Miracle Sales Guide. Englewood Cliffs, NJ: Prentice-Hall Inc., 1974.

Robertson, James. *Future Work*. New York: Universe Books, 1985.

Sales Manpower Foundation. *How to Land the Job You Want*. New York: Sales Executive Club of New York, 1975.

Sandhusen, Richard L. *Marketing*. New York: Barron's, 1987.

Schuller, Robert H. *You Can Become the Person You Want to Be*. New York: Pillar Books, 1973.

Shafiroff, Martin D. and Robert L. Shook. *Successful Telephone Selling in the 80's*. New York: Harper & Row, 1982.

Shatzki, Michael and Wayne R. Coffey. *Negotiating: The Art of Getting What You Want*. New York: New American Library, 1981.

Sher, Barbara and Annie Gottlieb. *Wishcraft: How to Get What You Really Want*. New York: Ballantine Books, 1979.

Shook, Robert L. *Telephone Selling Techniques that Really Work*. London: Piatkus, 1991.

Smith, Robert Ellis. *Workrights*. New York: E.P. Dutton, 1983.

Snelling, Robert O. *The Right Job*. New York: Penguin Books, 1987.

Snelling Robert O. and Anne M. Snelling. *Jobs! What They Are . . . Where They Are . . . What They Pay . . .* New York: Fireside Books, 1985.

Sperber, Philip. *The Science of Business Negotiation*. New York: Pilot Industries, 1979.

Walther, George R. *Phone Power: How to Make the Telephone Your Most Profitable Business Tool*. New York: Berkely Books, 1986.

Weinstein, Robert V. *Jobs for the 21st Century*. New York: Macmillan Publishing Co., 1983.

Welch, Mary Scott. *Networking: The Great New Way for Women to Get Ahead*. New York: Harcourt Brace Jovanovich, Inc., 1980.

Willingham, Ron. *Integrity Selling*. Garden City, NY: Doubleday & Co., 1987.

Yate, Martin John. *Great Answers to Tough Interview Questions*. London: Kogan Page, 1988.

Sources of company
information

CBI UK Kompass: The Authority on British Industry
Dunn & Bradstreet: Key British Enterprises
Macmillan's Unquoted Companies: Financial Profiles of Britain's Top 20,000
  Unquoted Companies
Macmillan Directory of Business Information Sources
The Hambro Company Guide
The Hambro Corporate Register: The Who's Who of Corporate Britain
The International Stock Exchange Official Yearbook
Local directories of industry and commerce

POSTSCRIPT

If you want to know more about Dorothy Leeds' speeches, seminars, and audiocassette programmes, please call or write to:

Dorothy Leeds, President
Organizational Technologies Inc.
Suite 10A
800 West End Avenue
New York, NY 10025
0101 (212) 864-2424
Fax 0101 (212) 932 8364

INDEX